Infamous Occasions

Infamous Occasions

*Being an Examination of Some Famous Racing
Scandals and Sensations Down the Ages*

JOHN WELCOME

MICHAEL JOSEPH

London

First published in Great Britain by
Michael Joseph Limited
44 Bedford Square, London W.C.1
1980

ⓒ 1980 by John Welcome

ISBN 0 7181 1810 3

Composition by Alacrity Phototypesetters,
Banwell, Avon, and printed and bound
in Great Britain by Billing & Sons Limited,
Guildford, London and Worcester

Contents

List of Illustrations

Acknowledgements

The chapter entitled 'Admiral Rous and the Tarragona Affair' first appeared in *The British Racehorse* and the author would like to thank the Editor for permission to reproduce it in this book.

The author would also like to thank *The British Racehorse* for providing the illustrations of Sir Charles Bunbury and Sam Chifney, the BBC Hulton Picture Library for the illustrations of the Earl of Durham and Sir George Chetwynd, and the Courtauld Institute of Art for the illustration of the Prince of Wales (later George IV) which is a painting by Gainsborough and hangs in Waddesdon Manor, Buckinghamshire.

Introduction

HISTORIANS SELDOM AGREE and the science of history is an inexact one, both of which facts provide much of the fascination which research and interpretation hold for those who wish to explore the events of the past and the characters who created them. Turf history is perhaps more inexact than most, since much of it is founded on personal recollections written long after the events recorded actually took place. Many recollections are ghosted, permitting a third party to interpose his views between writer and reader and therefore to some extent impairing the accuracy and impugning the authority of the finished product.

Much of Turf history, too, has been set down not in tranquillity but with a view to personal justification, to fulfilling old friendships or, on occasion, to paying off old scores. Many of the writers of these recollections — or their ghosts — took few pains to check their sources. Coming as most of them did from the upper, educated classes, the views and opinions expressed were, inevitably, those of their class and kind whose standards, such as they were (for until comparatively recently law of the jungle prevailed on the Turf and both rulers and ruled lived by it), they were at pains to protect and whose conduct they took care to justify. Thus myth and mistake proliferated.

Research and investigation revealed — at least to me — that many of these myths, propagated mostly by those who wielded power and adopted by their acolytes, had been accepted as truth and as such had passed as history down the years. Nor were those who attempted to challenge them popular and often, if they were connected with the sport, they put their livelihoods at risk, as did the unfortunate Argus in the Tarragona case, whom Admiral Rous had warned off the Turf without a hearing for daring to criticise him and then failing to tender an apology

11

when demanded. Allison, too, put himself in some peril of incurring the Duke of Westminster's wrath in the Orme poisoning case and only escaped by some astute manoeuvring and rapid covering of his tracks. In both these instances Argus and Allison were almost certainly right but their views are not those recorded by conventional history.

A more flagrant case in point is that of Lord George Bentinck. For years after his death he was held up as the very model of a Turf administrator — upright, honest, courageous and incorruptible, the terror of wrong-doers, the scourge of the wicked and the protector of the innocent. Old William Day started the rot and startled the few who read his memoirs — ghosted, of course — with his revelations, but no one took them very seriously. Day was only a trainer, then regarded as little better than a groom, and his book abounded in inaccuracies — he insisted, for instance, that the race which led to the Bentinck-Osbaldeston duel took place at Croxton Park, not Heaton Park. Many of his reminiscences of Bentinck were second-hand and his feelings towards him could easily be shown to be inspired by personal malice.

But when Lord George's own cousin, George Greville, took a hand it was an altogether different matter. Greville was the one-time racing confederate of Lord George; he was a highly intelligent man, he had been private secretary to the Secretary of State for War, and his position in society was every bit as secure as his cousin's. His animadversions and accusations, his revelations of the Turf idol's feet of clay, could not be taken lightly. Yet when his diaries containing them, together with much else, were published after his death they were greeted by the sporting and political establishment of the day with howls of execration. Disraeli, who had been Bentinck's patron and protector in Parliament, called them a 'political outrage'; Lord Winchilsea declared that they resembled 'the lives of the twelve Apostles written by Judas Iscariot'; Queen Victoria expressed herself to be shocked and horrified.

It was all an outburst of hypocrisy inspired by the desire to protect the façade, however sham, and avert the eyes from the horrid things that lurked behind it. But Greville set the record right, for he knew his cousin better than any man. Writing in his diary, and not then contemplating publication, he recorded the following judgment: 'The world will never know anything of these serious blemishes which could not fail to dim the lustre of his character.' The world, thanks to Greville, does know now. Had it not been for him, Bentinck would have passed into history as a sort of Bayard (though who, in fact, knows anything of Bayard's private life?) *sans peur et sans reproche*, a falsification if ever there was one.

Osbaldeston's reminiscences, discovered in the 1920s, might have done a little, even without Greville's memoirs, to dissipate the myths which had grown up around Lord George. Certainly they would have helped to set out the true facts surrounding the duel, about which so many versions exist that it is even now exceedingly difficult to separate fact from fiction. I believe the explanation I have suggested for its extraordinary outcome is the one most likely to be in accordance with the facts. The reason, I suggest, for the bias against Osbaldeston in most accounts springs from either sycophancy or a reluctance inspired by the public projection of his character to believe that anything could 'dim the lustre' of someone so apparently Bayard-like as Lord George.

It is sometimes said that if the Osbaldeston affair showed Bentinck at his worst or very near it, the Running Rein case and his exposure of the propagators of this fraud was a demonstration of his finest qualities. That Bentinck initiated and carried through reforms in racing urgently needed if the sport was to be rescued from permanent blackguardism, no one can deny. That in the Running Rein case he displayed the highest qualities of determination, dedication, and assiduous pursuit of wrong-doing in his resolve to bring the miscreants to book is also true. Unfortunately, even there he had recourse to methods above and beyond the law — he inspired, even if he did not himself carry out, the abduction of the real Running Rein from Goodman's stable so that the horse could not be produced before the judge. No doubt he considered himself above the law and that the ends justified the means — if the ends and the means were his.

I have not included a chapter on the Running Rein case — it seemed to me that since so much has already been written about it there is little left to say, whereas for the other events recorded here I have endeavoured to make a fresh interpretation of formerly accepted fact, to recount criminal or other instances not fully reported before or, as in the case of the 1913 Derby, to take another look at a much written-upon sensation in view of information that has recently come to light.

In doing this it has been forcibly brought home to me that one characteristic which runs through all these cases, except the criminal ones which were inspired by thirst for quick and unearned profit, is that of lust for power. Seldom have there been stronger examples of the truth of Acton's famous dictum that power corrupts and absolute power corrupts absolutely. Baldwin paraphrased this when he referred to 'power without responsibility, the prerogative of the harlot throughout the ages'. Much as they would have resented the comparison, harlotry was what those eminent gentlemen were committing when they misused for personal or other motives the absolute power thrust into their hands. Bunbury and Bentinck both used power for their own ends. Even Rous, an honourable and decent man at the outset of his long dictatorship, allowed himself to be so far corrupted as to act as he did in the Tarragona case. Loder, the sole arbiter, as it turns out, in the Craganour objection, decided as he did, or so it seems on the evidence, from suspect motives — though it should be stressed that absolute proof of this can never be given. What does seem clear from the evidence is that the decision was the wrong one, too hastily arrived at, and that the enquiry was not properly constituted according to the rules.

In the close-knit social structure which existed right up to World War II personal and family feuds flourished and proliferated far more than they do today. The leisured classes, who were then far more numerous, had time on their hands — they met more often and were thrown more closely together. The wounded and the wielder of the knife had such frequent encounters that to forget became impossible and constant reminders of wrongs, real or imagined, turned dislike on many occasions into real hatred. In turn this hatred spawned injustice.

Chetwynd was a victim, I suggest, not only of Durham's genuine drive for reform but also of something that lurked behind it, and of the Establishment's desire for a scapegoat. Virtually none of the offences with which he was charged were brought home to him and he deserved a better hearing than he received. Incidentally he did not, as is sometimes said, leave England after the verdict to live permanently in Monte Carlo. He continued to reside in London, wintering in Monte Carlo as he had always done.

The other side of racing — the seamier one — is exemplified in the three criminal cases I have looked at: Palmer the Poisoner, the Great Turf Frauds and the Coat of Mail case. Palmer was a cold-blooded killer by poison, a gambler, a forger and a thief. Yet, paradoxically, there has always been doubt as to whether he was properly convicted. The court was against him, the prosecuting counsel was determined for his own ends and his ambitions that he should hang; he was weakly defended and there was then no court of criminal appeal. Today, on the evidence as presented by the Crown, he might well have gone free.

The Great Turf Frauds show how clever and unscrupulous criminals can with persistence and a little luck subvert authority and how greed can conquer commonsense. They also show that police corruption is not confined to our own times. In the Coat of Mail case that engaging rogue Peter Christian Barrie drove a coach and four through the lax regulations of the twenties — regulations, incidentally, which Durham, despite his reputation as a Turf reformer and administrator, had done little or nothing to tighten up.

So there it is — power and money, the twin themes which govern much of life and which run continually and consistently through the episodes examined, I hope freshly, in this book.

CHAPTER 1

Royalty in Trouble:
The Escape Scandal and the
Prince of Wales

BOTH ON THE TURF and off it dictators are a danger to themselves and everyone else. The future George IV when Prince of Wales was to discover this to his cost.

Thomas Charles Bunbury, sixth baronet of Barton Hall, Bury St Edmund's, in the county of Suffolk, was the first great dictator of the Turf, 'perpetual president' of the Jockey Club for upwards of forty years, and a man whose word and writ were racing law. The baronetcy had been created in 1681 by Charles II. Sir Charles succeeded in 1764 at the age of twenty-two. Like his forebears he was a Whig; he was also a man of some culture, a close friend of Horace Walpole, Dr Johnson and Charles James Fox. On attaining his majority he had been elected Member of Parliament for Mildenhall, a constituency he continued to represent for almost the whole of his long life. A poor and fumbling speaker — 'a chicken orator', Walpole called him — he failed to cut much of a figure in debate, although he gave what weight he had to the campaign for the abolition of the slave trade.

Two years before he succeeded to the baronetcy Bunbury married Sarah, daughter of the second Duke of Lennox, an event which was to have a lasting effect on his life and character. Lady Sarah Lennox was a raving beauty with whom George III had fallen head over heels in love when she was a mere girl, but social and political influences prevented a marriage taking place. She appears to have married Bunbury on the rebound and to have been bored with him from the first. She thought him dull, tedious and a hypochondriac. 'He has to be ill,' she wrote to a friend. Five years after the marriage she left him and never returned, finally settling down with the Hon. George Napier and becoming the mother of the famous Napier soldier brothers. She was able to marry Napier since, nine years after their parting, Sir Charles divorced her, though in order to do so he had to obtain an Act of Parliament which was necessary for divorce in those days.

The whole affair of the marriage and its break-up was a scandal and a continuing one. Its cause and its consequences cannot but have had a traumatic effect on Bunbury. It seems, too, that Lady Sarah had not spared him in comparing him with her first and royal suitor. He would not have been human had his feelings towards the Royal Family remained untinged with resentment, and these feelings almost certainly played a considerable part in determining the attitude he took up when the greatest racing scandal of the age burst about the ears of society.

From his earliest youth Bunbury had displayed an interest in horses and racing, and almost as soon as he inherited he began to assemble a stud. The family seat was only a few miles from Newmarket, the home of racing, and within a few years his colours — pink and white stripes and black cap — were being successfully sported not only there but at other meetings throughout the country. Soon he was elected a member of the Jockey Club. Perhaps to compensate for his failures in Parliament and matrimony he threw himself heart and soul into its deliberations and debates and the administration of racing, such as it was then. In 1768, at the age of twenty-eight, he was nominated Steward of the Club. At that time there was only one steward, and even though the Club had not then appropriated to itself the plenary and absolute powers it was later to do, the person nominated was, nevertheless, in a position of immense authority. Two years later the system of electing three stewards and rotating them was adopted, but by this time Bunbury's domination was unassailable and he remained, as has been said, 'perpetual president' and in sole and absolute control of racing for the rest of his life.

The story has often been told of how the original conditions of the Derby and the Oaks sprang from Bunbury's mind, and of how he and Lord Derby tossed to see whose name should be given to the great race. Although Bunbury lost the toss he won the first running of the Derby with his colt Diomed. Before he died he was to win it twice more, with Eleanor and Smolensko. Eleanor, a filly, was the first of her sex to win both the Derby and the Oaks, and Smolensko was the first colt to win both the 2,000 Guineas and the Derby. If he was not the originator of it, Bunbury certainly encouraged the introduction of two-year-old racing. He also instigated the carrying of lighter weights and racing over shorter distances than the two or four miles almost universal at that time. There was no lack of critics, however — Nimrod amongst them — ready to suggest that his real reason for supporting this reform was that the blood in his own breed was not stout enough to win over the longer distances. In addition Bunbury was in favour of a much less severe system of training than prevailed then, condemning the 'strong sweats' advocated by the Days, the Chifneys and others.

Although he had been concerned with horses all his life he showed little sympathy or understanding of them. He sold one of his greatest servants on the racecourse, Diomed, at the age of twenty-three for fifty guineas to America. His loss was America's gain, for Diomed lived to be thirty-one and proved one of the greatest sires in American history. Bunbury was suspicious of his jockeys and niggardly with them; he was inclined to blame them unfairly in defeat and reward them parsimoniously in victory. Nimrod recalls how, when he was putting up Goddison on Smolensko before the Derby, Bunbury said to him: 'Here is your horse, Tom; he will do *his* duty, if you will do *yours*!'

The running of his horses, too, was not always above suspicion. Bellario and Sorcerer were two whose form was considered inconsistent. Even the great Diomed, the year after his

Derby victory, caused eyebrows to be raised in some quarters when, with odds of 4—1 laid on him, he was beaten by Fortitude at Nottingham. In the context of the times these occasions of in-and-out running would hardly call for comment, were it not for Bunbury's attitude and actions when he found himself on a collision course with the Prince of Wales and his jockey over the running of Escape at Newmarket in 1791. By that time Bunbury had reigned supreme on the Turf for many years. He was successful, dominant, unopposed, and he did not take kindly to opposition or competition — especially when the competition came from an unexpected and unwanted source: royalty.

In 1784 the Prince of Wales started his career on the Turf. Until he set up his own establishment in 1780 the Prince had been subjected by his father to an absurdly rigorous, restrictive and over-disciplined system of education and upbringing which included frequent flogging for the most minor offences. It was designed to fit the future occupant of the throne for the responsibilities of kingship. Inevitably it did nothing of the sort. Once he was free, like several of his descendants after him, he cast off the shackles with a vengeance. Dr Johnson's stanzas addressed to one of the Prince's greatest friends, Sir John Lade, on attaining his majority, might well have been written for him:

> Call the Betseys, Kates, and Jennies,
> All the names which banish care;
> Lavish of your grandsire's guineas,
> Show the spirit of an heir!
>
> Loosen'd from the minor's tether,
> Free to mortgage or to sell,
> Wild as wind and light as feather,
> Bid the sons of thrift farewell!

The Prince needed no injunction to 'bid the sons of thrift farewell'. He spent prodigiously but not, as it happened, unsuccessfully where hunters or racehorses were concerned. He tried all the hacks and hunters personally. They were brought to him by Milton, his favourite dealer, with the exhortation to: 'Throw your thigh over him, your Highness, and you'll find him the sweetest goer you ever mounted.' This he would do enthusiastically, and although he may frequently have paid too much he seldom bought a bad one.

At this time of his life the Prince was far from being the corpulent and dissipated figure of scorn depicted by later cartoonists. He was tall and handsome and, when racing, turned out in the height of sporting fashion — 'blue coat with gilt buttons, top-boots and buckskins' — as advised by his friend Beau Brummell. He was a tremendously attractive man and, on the racecourse or off it, he charmed everyone he met.

That he kept raffish company and enjoyed it, again like certain of his descendants, cannot be denied. Sir John Lade, already mentioned, was perhaps his closest friend. Sir John was one of the best whips in the kingdom but even he could not match the skill of his wife, Letty. Lady Lade was beautiful but far from high-born. Before her marriage to Sir John she had been the mistress of a highwayman, Sixteen String Jack, who ended his career on the gallows at Tyburn. Also among the Prince's entourage were the notorious Barrymore brothers, 'Hellgate', 'Cripplegate' and 'Newgate', together with their sister whom the Prince himself delightedly christened 'Billingsgate' after listening to the ripe and full-flavoured language which flowed from her lips. It is not surprising that when the Prince of Wales invaded Newmarket in the prime of his youth, surrounded by these flamboyant and disreputable characters, that Bunbury and others should take offence. When the Prince opened a ball at Brighton by dancing with Letty Lade, four well-born ladies — one of whom, however, married a hairdresser and was later imprisoned for debt — walked out of the room.

Despite all this, his worst offence in the eyes of the Establishment appears to have been that he was immediately and tremendously successful. On 8 May 1784 he had his first winner, a horse called Hermit. In the morning, when ridden by Mr

Thomas Panton (who was later to be one of those sitting in judgment in the Escape case) he was beaten in a match over a mile. That afternoon, however, professional jockeys were put up and the match repeated. This time Hermit won. The Prince went from strength to strength, winning the Derby in 1788 with Sir Thomas — he was the first member of the royal house to do so.

The years between, however, were not without their vicissitudes. If he fancied a horse he bought it, regardless of cost, and, like his associates, he gambled recklessly. His racing stable, which had started in 1784 with four horses, rapidly increased to forty. In 1786 he had twenty-five horses in training at Newmarket alone, and his gambling and other debts amounted to over £160,000. That year he had a right royal row with his father and Parliament over his extravagances and he was forced to cut back. He sold off his racehorses and dispersed his stud.

The retrenchment did not last long. By 1788 he and his raffish friends had returned to Newmarket and he had started to rebuild his string. Then began such a run of royal winners as has never been seen before or since on the English Turf. In the four years between 1788 and 1792 he won 185 races including a Derby and eighteen King's Plates. The stakes amounted to over £30,000. No wonder envious eyes were cast at his success, crowned by his Derby win in 1788; and he cannot have enhanced his popularity with Bunbury by frequently employing as his jockey Sam Arnhill, who had won Bunbury his first Derby on Diomed and whom Bunbury looked upon as his personal property.

Some years earlier Bunbury had bred a colt, Highflyer, whom he sold and in so doing lost a fortune, for Highflyer proved a prepotent and immensely successful sire. The Prince had bred from him a colt which was sold to a Mr Franco on his dispersal sale. When he returned to racing the Prince remembered that this Highflyer colt had caught his eye. He went to Mr Franco and bought him back for £15,000. While in Mr Franco's ownership the colt had put his leg through the side of his box and been trapped there. The stud-groom had managed to free him without injury and, on hearing the story, Mr Franco had named the colt Escape.

The purchase of Escape was in some ways the best, but, in its final result, unquestionably the worst, investment in bloodstock the Prince ever made. At first it seemed that Escape would prove himself an outstanding racehorse. Indeed, at his best, as Sam Chifney said later on, he was well-nigh unbeatable. But, as he was to show, he was far from always at his best. He had two ways of running and no one knew from one day to the next whether he would decide to put it all in and win his race or trail home disinterestedly at the back of the field. In addition he had a delicate constitution, did not hold his condition, and was difficult to train. But he ran and won for the Prince just the same as did many others and, with his string and his successes increasing, the Prince felt he must employ a permanent jockey. His choice fell on Samuel Chifney the Elder.

Chifney was, without any shadow of doubt, one of the great jockeys of all time. His hands were so light that he described his own method of riding a racehorse as 'if you had a silken rein as fine as a hair in his mouth and were afraid of breaking it'. Not only did he have superb hands but his judgment of pace was unrivalled. The 'Chifney rush', by which he would suddenly gather up his horse some strides from the finish and touch off an opponent by half a length, is said to have been perfected by his son, young Sam, but he invented it.

The Prince took an immediate fancy to Chifney, gave him a retainer of £200 a year, and made him something of a court favourite. He would walk for hours with him up and down the Steine at Brighton, deep in conversation about his horses and their chances. His worth to the royal stable was soon proved on a desperate puller called Knowsley which the Prince purchased for £1,000. No other jockey had been able to hold him or manage him. On each previous outing he had run himself into the ground and been beaten. He was entered in the King's Plate at Guildford and the Prince and his companions came down to watch him run and see what would happen to Chifney. When the jockey arrived at the stable the groom offered him the fearsome curb bit which had been used in Knowsley's mouth in his previous races. 'Take that silly gimcrack thing away and bring me a plain snaffle,' Chifney said. The groom did as he was told and Chifney won by three lengths with Knowsley going docilely on a slack rein. He repeated his win a few days later, to the Prince's delight.

But there can be little doubt that these attentions from royalty went to Chifney's head. He became thoroughly conceited and aired his opinions too freely for his own good. Chifney had always held a high opinion of himself and his abilities, which he later expressed thus: 'In 1773 I could ride horses in a better manner in a race than any person ever known in my time, and in 1775 I could train horses for running better than any person I ever yet saw.' It is not surprising that he had positive ideas about the training and placing of the Prince's horses, and it was almost inevitable that he should fall out with Mr Warwick Lake, the racing manager, and Neale, the trainer. Moreover, though he paid lip-service to Bunbury's theories about the benefits of a milder system of training, in private he continued to advocate the 'heavy sweating' of horses two or three times a week.

All these things combined to increase the jealousy and disapproval with which the Prince, his servants and his friends were regarded by the 'perpetual president' of the Jockey Club and his acolytes, whose achievements he had outshone and of whose opinions and rules of propriety he was openly disdainful. As always throughout his life he avoided the staid and the boring. Yet, while admitting into his intimate circle anyone whom he liked or who amused him, he let it be known that he remained conscious of his position as First Gentleman of Europe. Those who presumed too far did so at their peril, and those who attempted to claim an acquaintanceship he did not desire were ruthlessly snubbed. None of this enhanced his popularity with the racing hierarchy. No wonder, then, that H. H. Dixon, 'The Druid', a respected sporting historian of the mid-nineteenth century, made no bones about the attitude towards him of Sir Charles Bunbury and his like. 'There is very little doubt', he wrote, 'that nothing but rank jealousy of the popularity which he acquired, caused a few Turf rivals to join in the dead set that drove him from Newmarket.'

Matters came to a head over the running of Escape at the Newmarket October meeting of 1791. At the Ascot meeting the same year Escape had given an example of his in-and-out running. The Prince had four horses entered in the Oatlands Stakes, then the richest race in England — Baronet, Escape, Pegasus and Smoker. Five days before the race the four of them were tried over the Oatlands distance, carrying the weights they would have in the race. Escape, giving Baronet 20lb, beat him by a neck. It was a very severe trial, and when Chifney saw Escape again on the morning of the race he felt that the horse had not recovered from it. Accordingly he asked the Prince if he could ride Baronet instead. Lake, the racing manager, and Neale, the trainer, were also present and they did not agree with Chifney. An argument ensued to which the Prince put an end by saying: 'Whenever I have two horses in a race I wish you, Sam, to ride the one you fancy most on the day without consulting us about it.'

Nineteen of the best horses in England faced the starter. At the line, chiefly through Chifney's brilliance, Baronet won a hard-fought battle by half a length. Escape finished well down the field. Chifney's judgment was borne out and the Prince was so delighted that he had a portrait of Baronet with Chifney in the saddle painted by Stubbs.

When the Newmarket October meeting came round Escape was again due to run. He was entered for two races, the first on 20 October being over the Ditch In course of two miles, and the second, the following day, over the Beacon course of four miles.

Once again before the race there was an argument about Escape's chances. Chifney maintained that the horse was short of a gallop and would not win. If Lake and Neale were indignant about this they had some justification, for it was admitted on all sides that Escape was difficult to train — at Ascot Chifney had blamed them for putting too much work into him, and now Chifney appeared to be saying that they had given him too light a preparation. Chifney, however, advised the Prince not to back him and did not back him himself (jockeys in those days were allowed to bet).

On the day of the first race Escape was opposed by three other horses. None of them was of much account and he was made favourite at 2—1. It appears that he was heavily backed by most of the nobility and gentry present at the meeting. He never got into the race at all and finished last. In view of what was to happen it is worth giving the actual result:

Mr Dawson's Coriander	1.
Lord Grosvenor's Skylark	2.
Lord Clermont's Pipator	3.
HRH The Prince of Wales's Escape	4.

There the matter might have rested had not Escape been pulled out again the following day to run over the Beacon course. There were six runners including Pipator and Skylark, who had both beaten him the day before. The Duke of Bedford's Grey Diomed, held to be the best horse by Diomed bred in England, and another useful horse, Lord Barrymore's Chanticleer, were also entered. Altogether it was a much higher-class field than that of the previous day but it must be remembered that the race was over a different course and a longer distance, and that Escape was a stayer.

In view of the former result it is not surprising that the odds against Escape went out to 5—1. Chanticleer was favourite at 7—4. In the race Escape, waited with and coming with a run at the finish, did everything he was asked to do and won easily. The finishing order was:

HRH The Prince of Wales's Escape	1.
Lord Barrymore's Chanticleer	2.
Lord Grosvenor's Skylark	3.
Duke of Bedford's Grey Diomed	4.
Lord Clermont's Pipator	5.
Mr Barton's Alderman	6.

It will be seen that not only had Escape beaten the favourite, Chanticleer, and also Grey Diomed, but that the two horses Skylark and Pipator, who had finished in front of him the day before, gave almost exactly the same running in this race.

Uproar followed. Here was the chance that the Prince's rivals and denigrators, led by Bunbury, were looking for. The wildest stories were put about, one of them being that the Prince had visited the stables just before the first race and had himself given Escape a bucket of water to affect his wind. Lake, the racing manager, did not hesitate to add fuel to the flames, going to the Prince and suggesting strongly that Chifney had stopped the horse when he was beaten on the first day. When he heard this Chifney went in search of the Prince and demanded that Lake should either substantiate his allegations of withdraw them.

But by then Bunbury, too, had been busy and was calling for a full investigation into the whole matter. It was Chifney's riding which was ostensibly the subject of the enquiry, but everyone knew that the real target was the Prince himself, who was said — inaccurately — to have won thousands over the second race. Moreover it had not escaped attention that the beaten favourite was owned by Lord Barrymore, one of his closest friends.

The next day the Prince sent for Chifney and questioned him closely on his riding and his betting in the two races. Appearing satisfied by his answers, he then asked Chifney if he would swear an affidavit setting out these answers in full and if he was prepared to appear before the Jockey Club. Chifney sturdily replied that he was prepared to appear before anyone.

Before racing the next day Bunbury accosted the Prince on the matter. No record of the conversation exists but he appears to have demanded instant condemnation of Chifney by the Prince, which the Prince refused to give. Then, seeing Chifney standing some distance away, the Prince beckoned him over. Their horses were sent for and all three went together out on to the Heath, presumably to avoid any possibility of eavesdropping. The Prince instructed Chifney to ride between himself and Bunbury, who proceeded to discuss the matter across him, the Prince affirming his belief in his innocence and Bunbury refusing to accept it. Finally the Prince turned to Chifney and said: 'Sam Chifney, I think you told me that you were willing to be examined by the stewards of the Jockey Club in any way they should think proper?'

'Your Royal Highness, I am proud to meet any man on the subject,' was Chifney's reply.

'There, Sir Charles,' the Prince then said. 'You hear him say he is proud to meet any man on the subject. Now, Sir Charles, I beg of you to take every pains so as to make yourself perfectly satisfied; and then enclose me Sam Chifney's affidavit, and apprise me how the business ends.

Chifney duly swore his affidavit and was summoned to appear before the stewards of the Jockey Club — Sir Charles Bunbury, Mr Thomas Panton, and Mr Ralph Dutton. It is hardly necessary to say that Bunbury presided. To place oneself in the position of prosecutor and judge at one and the same time, which is what Bunbury did, makes the administration of justice, even with the best will in the world, exceedingly difficult. When bias enters in, as it did here, it becomes all but impossible.

Bunbury, it is clear, was determined to deal out retribution to Chifney and through him to the Prince. The other two stewards took little or no part in the enquiry. Bunbury ran it, turning himself into a prosecutor of the utmost severity, harassing Chifney and cross-examining him at length about his bets and his manner of riding.

Chifney stood by his affidavit and maintained that what he had said in it was the truth. He pointed out, too, Escape's known tendency to run no two races the same, that he was short of a gallop in the first race and, insofar as he was allowed to with the dictator of the Turf thundering at him, that the two races were over different courses and distances and that Escape had shown his best form as a stayer. All this must have taken some courage and strength of character when one takes into consideration the social climate of the times, the differing levels of education of the two men, and the weight of authority behind Bunbury.

After the enquiry closed no official statement of its findings was issued by the stewards, nor was any formal censure or reprimand given to Chifney, but Bunbury let it be widely known that he was far from satisfied with Chifney's explanations. Shortly afterwards, apparently acting entirely on his own initiative, he sent the Prince of Wales a message that if he

28

permitted Chifney to continue to ride his horses no gentleman would start against him.

By any standards this was an extraordinary communication for one of his future subjects to address to the heir to the throne. Bunbury, too, though he may have constituted himself un-crowned king of the Turf, was a mere baronet off the Turf, occupying the lowest step in the aristocratic ladder. The Prince was outraged, and rightly so.

The Prince of Wales, as his later career was to show, had many faults and weaknesses of character. But he never forgot a friend, and never betrayed a trust once given, nor the loyalty of a servant. As has been frequently pointed out, he could then have avoided all further discussion on the case and his own possible implication by disavowing Chifney and disassociating himself from him. This he refused to do. His response was dignified, immediate and irreversible. He informed Bunbury that if he or any member of the Jockey Club could prove that Chifney had committed a fraud he would dismiss him forthwith and never employ him again. Failing that the jockey would continue to carry his colours and his trust. If Bunbury refused either to substantiate or retract, rather than disown Chifney and so convict him by this action he would abandon racing and Newmarket altogether.

Neither Bunbury nor any member of the Jockey Club could in fact prove that Chifney had cheated. All the evidence when dispassionately surveyed pointed the other way. But Bunbury, in his privileged position as dictator would not put himself in the wrong by retracting. Obstinate and overbearing, he seems to have believed that the Prince would not have the stomach to stand up to him. If so, it was a grave error of judgment and reflects poorly on Bunbury's ability to assess character.

For the royal mind was made up. He refused to budge from the stance he had taken. Shortly afterwards he left Newmarket, never to return. Over the coming months he sold off all his horses and by December of the following year he had left the Turf, apparently forever. Before doing so he summoned Chifney to his presence and affirmed his belief in his innocence and integrity. He went on to tell him that he was unlikely ever to keep or race horses again but: 'If I do so, Sam Chifney, you shall train and manage them. You shall have the two hundred guineas a year just the same. I cannot give it to you for your life, only for my own. You have been an honest and good servant to me.'

As might have been expected, once the royal patronage and protection on the Turf were taken from him Chifney was exposed to the full enmity of Bunbury and his ilk. Not un-naturally his career went into a decline. Some years after the affair he wrote a book with the curious title of *Genius Genuine* setting out his version of what had happened. Although it cost £5 — a substantial sum in those days — it was immediately popular and went into a second edition, showing that memories of Bunbury's misuse of power were still strong and that Chifney's name retained much of its former magic. Misfortune and his enemies still pursued him, however. He was forced to commute the Prince's pension for £1,200. Then he went to London with a new bit, 'The Chifney', which he had invented, intending to patent and market it. He lacked a head for business and the bit was not a financial success. As a result of a debt he had incurred in its production he was prosecuted and committed to the Fleet Prison. The rigours of life there affected his health and he died within its walls in 1807, aged fifty-two.

The Prince never forgave Bunbury or the Jockey Club. In 1805 a deputation led by Bunbury himself waited on him at the Pavilion in Brighton where he was staying. They informed him that the Club had passed a resolution in the following words: 'May it please your Royal Highness, the members of the Jockey Club deeply regretting your absence from Newmarket, earnestly intreat that the affair may be buried in oblivion, and sincerely hope that the different meetings may again be honoured by your Royal Highness's condescending attendance.'

As a retraction it came far too late. The Prince, affable as ever, heard them out courteously, said that he accepted the spirit in which the resolution had been passed, and that he would consider returning to Newmarket. He never did. Many years later, when he was on the throne, he resumed ownership of racehorses and ran them but never at Newmarket. He had not forgotten the Chifneys and employed Sam the Elder's two sons, William and Sam Junior, as his trainer and jockey. When it was suggested by William that the King should run one of his good horses at Newmarket he answered: 'No, no, William, they treated your poor father and me very badly. I won't run there.'

The extent of the sacrifice which the Prince made in standing by his jockey may be judged by the fact that horses and racing were the two things he truly loved. 'It was *horses, horses* with him by night and by day to the very last,' one of his physicians said of him in his final illness, and when he was dying he sent a messenger specially to Epsom with express instructions to return with the result of the Derby as soon as it was declared. The winner was William Chifney's Priam and, ill as the King was, he had it in mind to buy the winner for 3,500 guineas in a last effort to win the St Leger and credit himself with another classic race. It was not to be, for he died just over a month later.

No responsible source ever dared to suggest that George IV, during his long and successful career on the Turf, would for a moment have countenanced anything that smacked of cheating. The same could not be said of others who played principal parts in this sorry affair. Let Nimrod, the great sporting writer of the day, have the last word on it:

> But if the change to a certain extent in a horse's running is itself enough to damage the character of its owner, what would have become of that of his Royal Highness's principal accuser, the late Sir Charles Bunbury? Look at the running of his Eleanor: it is well known that she was the winner of both Derby and Oaks — the best mare of her day. Well! at Huntingdon she was beaten by a common plater, a mare called Two Shoes, *ten to one on Eleanor*. The next week at Egham, she beat a first-rate racehorse, Bobadil, and several others, *ten to one on Bobadil*. In both these cases money was lost, and the question that follows is, — who won it?

CHAPTER 2

Pistols in the Morning:
The Osbaldeston–Bentinck Duel

IF SIR CHARLES BUNBURY was a dictator and a dangerous one, Lord George Bentinck, who followed him as supreme arbiter of the Turf, was even more domineering, more autocratic and wielded more absolute power. Many theories have been put forward to explain the character of this extraordinary man. He was a younger son — the third son of the fourth Duke of Portland — and it is said that he resented this position. Bentinck was a failure in the Army, in Parliament and in love — all his life he cherished a hopeless passion for the Duchess of Richmond — and it has been suggested that he could only prove himself to himself by success in the supreme councils of the Turf. A solitary education at the hands of tutors did not improve matters. It appears to have given him a feeling of inferiority compared with the products of the greater public schools, rendering him introspective and resentful of the standing and success of others and making him determined to surpass them. And there can be no doubt that, despite the hundred years of residence and preferment which his family had enjoyed in England, he still harboured within himself the Dutch qualities of giving too little and asking too much.

As with all complex human beings, no one explanation will suffice and to say that his character was an amalgam and distillation of all these traits is probably the best one is likely to achieve. Whatever strange genes combined to produce him, he remains one of the most disturbing and fascinating characters ever to tread the English Turf. During his lifetime he bestrode it like a Colossus. By his furious energy, his dedication, his unswerving pursuit of those whom he deemed to be malefactors likely to damage the image of racing he was trying to propagate, he made himself the most powerful and ruthless dictator the Turf has ever known.

Unfortunately he was devious. One set of rules existed for others; another for himself. A gambler on a heroic scale — 'He counted the thousands he won after a great race as a general would count his prisoners and cannon after a great victory' — he did not hesitate to manipulate the betting market to his own advantage by the most outrageous ruses, many of which came perilously close to fraud. His endeavours to conceal his ownership of racehorses and his betting from his father were unsuccessful and he was hauled over the parental coals. He gave a promise not to gamble again, but did not keep it. Each year his stratagems became more and more blatant. When his reputation as a Turf reformer was at its height his cousin George Greville wrote in his diary: 'What a humbug it all is, and if every one knew all I know of his tricks and artifices what a rogue he would be thought!'

He quarrelled with Greville as he quarrelled with everyone who did not bend to his arrogant will and acknowledge that he was above the law. Rude and domineering, aggressive in all he did, he was also unbearably vindictive. 'While there was nothing in the world he would not do to help a friend,' it was said of him by one who knew him well, 'he would go three times round the world to injure or defeat a foe.'

He almost seemed to go out of his way to demonstrate in public the unpleasant aspects of his character. On one occasion, when dining in his club, he saw the waiter bring the bill to another member, Sir St Vincent Cotton. Cotton was recuperating from a long and dangerous illness and, possibly for that reason, had been slow in settling some of his losing wagers. Lord George had a high-pitched, drawling voice which, when he desired it, lent even greater offence to words which were intended to hurt. He used it now, commanding the waiter to bring him Sir St Vincent Cotton's bill. Having glanced at it, he said in tones which carried throughout the coffee-room: 'Before Sir St Vincent Cotton orders such expensive dinners he should pay his debts of honour.'

'It was cruel and crushing and possibly well deserved,' Thormanby, the Turf historian, wrote of this incident, 'but was it quite the act of a gentleman?'

This arrogant behaviour, combined with a delight in giving offence to others, may well have hidden an insecurity engendered by his earlier failures and his continued lack of success in Parliament where *Punch*, for instance, guyed him unmercifully. 'Lord George is a-coming, huzza! huzza! He's prosing and summing, and hawing and humming — yes, that's him a-coming, huzza! huzza!' ran one stanza of the many verses devoted to satirizing his feeble performances. His fellow-members, too, taunted and twitted him. After one particularly incoherent and halting speech from his lips Sir James Graham scathingly referred to him as 'a great authority on the doctrine of chances', and the implied reference to his gambling was not lost on the House. In the actual pursuit of field sports and outdoor activity he proved himself to be an indifferent performer. He was a clumsy and awkward horseman, and his attempts at riding races proved so ludicrous that he soon abandoned them; he was far from a thruster out hunting, and was a poor shot.

None of these things deterred him from his policy of not swerving from his chosen course which was to become the ultimate authority in racing. Indeed it is probable that they spurred him on. Nor did they alter his character. In Parliament and out of it he continued to harry with merciless invective those who opposed him or who stood up to him. But when he indulged in this characteristic towards George Osbaldeston after the Heaton Park meeting in 1835 it very nearly cost him his life.

George 'Squire' Osbaldeston was, in character, the very antithesis of his adversary. A small, sturdy man — he stood a shade under five foot six inches in height and weighed eleven stone — his family motto was 'What man dare, I dare' and never was an escutcheon more bravely borne. He was above all a sportsman and it was as a sportsman — cricketer, shot, huntsman and race-rider — that he excelled. He was one of the six best amateur cricketers in England; he was the first com-moner to hunt the Quorn Hounds, where he showed superlative sport; he and a Captain Horatio Ross were rated the two best game shots in England; with a pistol he could put ten shots into the ace of diamonds at thirty paces. His feats as a gentleman rider both on the flat and over fences passed into legend. His biographer records of him:

> ... nearly everything he did was done as well as about any other living Englishman could do it.... In fact I do not wonder that most people were polite to a plucky little customer who kept his temper better than most people but who could either knock you down out of hand or put a bullet through your head next morning whichever he preferred. ... If he had to teach Gully manners by putting a bullet through his hat, it was with Gully that he dined after his famous match against Time, and with Gully he continued friendly relations as long as he was on the Turf.

Unlike Lord George, Osbaldeston was never known to nurse resentment or to keep up a quarrel. Creevey, the diarist, meeting him at a house-party and observing him closely as a type with which he had had little acquaintance, noted him as 'clever in his way, good-humoured and gay'.

Well indeed did he merit the sobriquet of 'The Squire of England', for he embodied nearly all of the traditional English manly virtues of the time. And, being the man he was, he was not given to taking insults lying down.

The Heaton Park races, sometimes called 'The Goodwood of the North', organised on behalf of Lord Wilton and held in the grounds of his Lancashire demesne, had for some years before 1835 been known to racing men as an aristocratic fraud. It was an accepted fact that Lord Wilton's horses, trained for him by John Scott, were thrown into the handicaps at ludicrously low weights to give them an unfair advantage and, worse, there was evidence that, in the event of a close finish involving one of His Lordship's horses, the judge had instructions to give the verdict in his favour. In each of the three years prior to 1835 either Lord Wilton's own horses or those trained by John Scott won eight of the ten races run at Heaton Park. The matter became something of an open scandal, so much so that many owners declined to run their horses for Lord Wilton's benefit and in 1834 he had been heard to complain that the entries had been greatly reduced. This did not deter him, however, from continuing to entertain the handicapper at his house-party for the races, and it did not escape comment that he was the sole official so honoured, since the company at the house was both aristocratic and exclusive. To cause even greater offence, Lord Wilton also continued his practice of granting only to his own trainer, John Scott, the privilege of training his horses in the park surrounding the house. All the owners and trainers were refused permission, leaving them with no option but to use the old Manchester racecourse which, as Osbaldeston commented, was then one of the worst and most waterlogged in England.

The matter had become such a scandal that some time before the date of the Heaton Park meeting in 1835 a meeting of owners and trainers was held in Manchester to consider ways of defeating the system and showing up the frauds perpetrated there. Osbaldeston, who ran horses constantly at Heaton Park but who was not included in the exclusive guest list at the mansion, attended it. A lengthy and heated discussion took place, and various schemes were propounded, none of which was considered satisfactory. Finally Osbaldeston got to his feet and told the assembled company that if they would leave it all to him he was sure he could find a way of exposing the injustices, especially the unfair handicapping.

He decided that he must get hold of a horse of whose capabilities the handicapper had no knowledge. There was only one place, he considered, where he could be sure of doing this, and that was Ireland. At that time Irish horses were, in general terms, thought to be at least a stone inferior to their English counterparts. Osbaldeston did not subscribe to that view, but it suited his plans very well for he knew that the handicapper regarded Irish form as valueless. Eventually he found one suited to his purpose — Rush, a four-year-old colt by Humphrey Clinker out of Wire. Rush had won several Queen's Plates and Osbaldeston judged him to be, in his own words, 'pretty smart'. About a week before the Doncaster races of 1835 he bought Rush for 400 guineas.

Rush duly arrived in England without any notice being taken of him and Osbaldeston proceeded to try him. On the morning of the St Leger he paid a trainer called Marson ten guineas for the use of a five-year-old mare whom he also knew to be 'pretty smart'. In the trial, which was to be over the full St Leger distance, he set Rush to give the mare 10lb. He rode Rush himself and put a professional up on the mare. The trial took place at six o'clock in the morning and, as they were going out, Marson told Osbaldeston that if Rush could beat the mare at those weights and with the difference in age against him he must be useful indeed.

The ground was heavy but Osbaldeston was determined to find out just what he had under him, and he instructed the jockey on the mare to make the gallop a strong one. After they had covered three-quarters of a mile Rush was still on the bit while the mare was all out. Osbaldeston went on and at a mile and a quarter was eight or nine lengths clear. At this point he spotted a group of people gathered at the winning-post, watching the trial. He eased Rush, with the result that the mare passed him and appeared to the onlookers to have won the trial as she liked. Rush's owner, however, knew he could have given the mare another stone and still beaten her. 'This', he observed laconically in his memoirs, 'made Rush a good horse, which he was.'

Lord George was one of those who attended Heaton Park races every year. He was a member of the house-party, amongst whom there was heavy betting on the outcome of the events and he, as usual, was one of the biggest plungers. His scouts were everywhere and it appears that the result of the trial, showing the mare a clear winner, was immediately conveyed to him. Heaton Park races were run a week after the St Leger meeting. Osbaldeston had entered Rush in the handicap, the Manchester Stakes, on the first day of the meeting, 24 September. Suspecting that something was afoot, Lord Wilton positioned his jockey, William Scott, down the course to observe the running and report on it. Since his own filly, Lady de Gros, was set to give Rush a stone in this race he had good reason for trying to find out just how good the colt was. The fact that he was under observation was conveyed to Osbaldeston by a friend from the house-party, and he took his own measures to confound the watchers.

There can be absolutely no doubt that Osbaldeston deliberately stopped Rush in this race. Indeed he admits it, but, being a consummate horseman, he did it with great skill; and, as he says in his memoirs, 'Rush was such a beautiful horse to ride they could not detect any "roping".' Rush finished last. Lady de Gros was well beaten by Whitefoot into second place. The result was so obvious that money was actually exchanging hands on Whitefoot when Orton, the judge, announced Lady de Gros as the winner. This announcement nearly caused a riot, and when Orton returned to Manchester that night he was lucky to avoid a lynching party.

The following day the chief race of the meeting, the Gold Cup, was to be run and both Rush and Lady de Gros were among the entries. When the handicapper declared the weights it was seen that he had accepted the previous day's form and had given Lady de Gros the task of conceding no less than 2st to Rush — the actual weights being Lady de Gros 12st 2lb and Rush 10st 2lb. Osbaldeston had well and truly achieved his object of humbugging the handicapper, and when he heard the weights he knew that he had indeed something to bet on. He entrusted his old friend, George Payne, with the commission.

Payne, one of the best-known and best-liked sportsmen of the day, was a compulsive and inveterate gambler. Inheriting a large fortune accumulated by careful trustees during a long minority, when at Oxford he had 'turned Christ Church into a hunting box'. Even the easy-going dons of the day could not in the end tolerate this, and he was asked to remove himself and his horses from the University. He then embarked on a lifetime of gambling with cards and horses so deeply and so recklessly and, it must be said, so unluckily, that in the end he lost everything including his ancestral home, Sulby Hall in Leicestershire, where he and Osbaldeston once played whist for £100 a trick and £1,000 the rubber. But he never lost the affection of his friends nor, for that matter, the admiration of the British public, who dearly love a gallant loser.

Payne was among the select few invited to stay at Heaton Park. The night before the race heavy gambling took place among the house-party on the result of the Gold Cup. Payne openly and with substantial sums supported Rush. Lord George, believing his observation of the previous day's running to be accurate and remembering the result of the trial which had been conveyed to him, just as heavily opposed him.

On the racecourse next day the market opened with Rush at 10—1. Payne went in and plunged so heavily on him that the odds tumbled. He did not scruple to take the cream of the market for himself, obtaining 10—1 for his own money before the odds shortened to 5—1, at which price he placed Osbaldeston's commission. Even that, however, was far better than the starting price, for the odds continued to fall until they reached 2—1.

Lord George could never be convinced by himself or anyone else that he might be wrong in his observations, opinions, deductions or actions. He had made up his mind that Rush was useless and that was that. The weight of money pouring in for Osbaldeston's colt from all quarters — for an Irish contingent had come over and was backing Rush frenetically — meant nothing to him. When the horses were actually on the racecourse and about to canter back to the start he called out in his high, neighing voice: 'Two to one against Rush!'

Osbaldeston, hearing him, called back from the saddle: 'Done! Put a hundred down to me.'

Before the start Osbaldeston took the precaution of going up to Orton who had been maintained in his position as judge despite the fracas of the day before. Drawing up his horse before the judge Osbaldeston said to him: 'Now, Orton, you see my colours distinctly?' When Orton replied that he did, Osbaldeston continued: 'Well, then, don't mistake one colour for another as you did yesterday, but I think you can't very easily as I shall win in a canter, and they are quite dissimilar.'

Osbaldeston's plan worked exactly as he had intended for he won in a common canter from Lord Wilton on Lady de Gros. His fellow gentleman-riders, to whom he had made no secret of his intentions, were highly delighted, but the aristocratic party was not so pleased. Lady Chesterfield and the Hon. Mrs Anson, heavy gamblers both, who had confidently supported Lady de Gros, hissed him as he passed the post, while both Lord Wilton and George Bentinck cut him dead in the weighing-room. However John Scott, Wilton's trainer, said to him as he returned to scale: 'Squire, you have done us this time.'

'Yes, Will,' was Osbaldeston's answer, 'and it is high time we should give you a rap on the knuckles to prove to you and the handicappers that we have seen through them for a long time and on this occasion we have helped ourselves.'

Lord George was coldly furious. One of his less endearing qualities was that he could not take a beating and, as he was to declare in Parliament later on, 'What I cannot bear is being sold.' He had been, he considered, sold on this occasion and by Squire Osbaldeston, a mere sporting commoner whose breeding and antecedents did not even qualify him for an invitation to the Wilton house-party. His indignation knew no bounds and was freely expressed over the port at Heaton Park that night. In taking up this attitude he overlooked the fact that, had he been as good a judge of racing as he considered himself, he should have appreciated that there was something false about Rush's earlier running, and had he been less set in his own opinions and more cautious in interpreting the odds, he would not have offered that bet so contemptuously to Osbaldeston.

Lord George was right to some extent in saying that he had been 'sold', for Osbaldeston had 'roped' Rush in the first race. However, taking into account the ethics of the day and the general air of fraud and double-dealing which surrounded the Heaton Park meeting, this would scarcely have been held against him had it not been for Lord George's strictures and loudly expressed condemnation. Indeed, compared to some of his own tricks and stratagems, what Osbaldeston did to him pales into insignificance, but Lord George could hardly have been expected to view it in that light.

Since he was then hunting six days a week, and cub-hunting the following morning, Osbaldeston had to leave Manchester immediately after the race. Before he went he asked George Payne to collect his £200 from Lord George. To his surprise and disappointment Payne replied that he had better do his collecting himself. Since Payne had won thousands on Rush and had not scrupled to collar the cream of Osbaldeston's market for himself, he does not come out of this very well, but then he was an easy-going man anxious to remain friends with everybody. He had heard Lord George's fulminations and no doubt had no wish to make himself a target for his cutting abuse. Osbaldeston spent the winter hunting and did not go racing again until the following spring, but he did not forget his debt.

At the Newmarket spring meeting, since Lord George had made no effort to settle in the meantime, Osbaldeston approached him. He found him 'standing in the betting yard with his back to the iron railings, looking very black, with a sort of savage smile on his countenance, not uncommon with him.'

'My Lord,' Osbaldeston said to him. 'I believe you owe me £200 which you lost to me on the Cup at Heaton Park.'

Lord George gave him one of his haughty stares and answered in his most carrying tones: 'I wonder you have the impudence and assurance to ask me for that money. A greater robbery was never committed by any man on the public; and the Jockey Club think so too.' This last comment was a flat mis-statement of fact, for the Jockey Club had held an informal enquiry but had taken no further action. However it is not unlikely that Lord George at that time considered himself to be the true embodiment of the Jockey Club and the sole interpreter of its rules and intentions. 'And', he continued, 'I have a great mind not to pay you at all.'

Osbaldeston had been openly insulted in public and he was not the man to let such an insult pass without the utterer paying

41

for it — most probably with his life. 'You must pay me,' he said. 'You don't think, My Lord, that the matter will end here. You will hear from me, and I beg you to understand that I consider myself quite as much of a gentleman as either you or any of the Jockey Club though I have not got a title attached to my name.'

'I suppose you can count,' Lord George said, contemptuously.

'I could at Eton,' was the reply, and in making it Osbaldeston must have known he would flick Lord George on the raw, for his sensitivity on the subject of his private and solitary education was well known.

Lord George then took a bundle of notes from his pocket, counted them out and paid his debt. But Osbaldeston was determined that the matter should not end there and promptly sought a second to support him in a duel. His first choice was George Payne, who had won a considerable sum on Rush himself. Osbaldeston was surprised and disappointed when Payne refused to act. Nor could he find anyone else at Newmarket who was prepared to stand for him. Finally, at his club in London, he obtained the consent of Colonel Dacre who, however, quickly changed his mind and withdrew. In his memoirs Osbaldeston says he could not understand the universal reluctance amongst his acquaintances to act as his second, but the reason is clear enough. He was probably the best pistol shot in England, while his opponent had hardly handled pistols in his life and certainly never in anger. Everyone believed Osbaldeston would kill Lord George, for he had declared his intention of doing so and he was not one to diverge from a course of action once his mind was made up. No one wanted to be associated with this killing.

Lord George was the third son of a ducal house whose social and political influence was enormous; in addition he was a Member of Parliament, which, despite his failure as a speaker, still gave him influence with those who wielded power. The storm which would ensue from his death in a duel was bound to be immense. Moreover, although the Duke, his father, had the reputation of being a mild and easy-going man, the Portlands were all good haters and he was not likely to take kindly to the killing of a son or to look with benevolence upon anyone associated with it. Compared to this array of wealth, power and privilege Osbaldeston was a mere sporting figure, a Master of Foxhounds, a commoner, prominent indeed in the sporting world but nowhere else.

At length Osbaldeston found a Mr Humphreys to act for him. Colonel Anson stood for Lord George and a meeting was arranged — or very nearly so, for at the last moment Lord George declined to face the Squire on the grounds that he was not a gentleman and his dignity therefore would not allow him to engage in a duel with one of a lower social order. This was exactly the same tactic that he had employed some years before when he had been called out by a brother officer in the Army, and it might well have led to accusations of cowardice had not his subsequent conduct amply given them the lie.

When this insulting information was conveyed to him by his second Osbaldeston instructed Humphreys to inform Colonel Anson that unless George Bentinck either apologised or faced him he would go to Tattersall's and there, in public, at the earliest opportunity, pull Lord George's long nose. The threat of this indignity and of being exposed as a laughing stock abruptly changed Bentinck's mind and he agreed to fight. His friends were aghast and sought desperately for some means of settling the dispute. It was then that George Payne, as a friend of both parties, took a further hand in the affair.

Payne hated duelling. His father had been killed in a duel by the brother of a young girl whom he had seduced. He was a man of peace and along with Colonel Anson, Bentinck's second, a known mediator. Payne and Anson attended on Lord George and endeavoured by every means they knew to prevail upon him to do something which would allow the matter to be settled both peaceably and with honour. After hours of discussion and argument he eventually agreed that they should draft a letter, the terms of which would hopefully satisfy the Squire and, if he approved of it when he saw it, he would sign it. Some time later they brought their draft to him in White's Club. He took it from them, read it through twice and carefully pondered its contents. Then he rose from his chair, tore the missive up and threw the pieces into the waste-paper basket. 'It's no use,' he told them. 'It was a robbery. Damn the fellow, I hate him and I won't withdraw a word.'

It appeared that he had sealed his fate, but Payne was not done with yet. Having failed with Lord George, he determined to seek out Osbaldeston. He found him, as he thought he would, playing whist at the Portland Club. He insisted on the Squire speaking to him alone as soon as the rubber was finished. Osbaldeston, who did not care for being interrupted at play, agreed with some reluctance, and since there was nowhere sufficiently private in the Club, the two men went down into the street. Payne employed all his skill in diplomacy and used every argument he could think of to persuade Osbaldeston not to kill Lord George. He found the Squire every bit as obdurate as his adversary. He had been publicly insulted, he said — as indeed he had — and nothing could settle it save an abject apology. 'It's no good, George,' he went on. 'He said it was a damned robbery, and as sure as you stand there I will shoot the beggar dead tomorrow morning, or rather, this morning for it's after midnight.'

At that Payne confessed himself defeated. Turning to Osbaldeston, he took his leave with the following words: 'Osbaldeston, you and I are old friends. You know Bentinck was right. It was a damned robbery;* and if you kill Lord George tomorrow there will not be a single gentleman in England who will ever speak to you again.'

According to Payne Osbaldeston stopped in his tracks, stared open-mouthed at him for a moment and then turned on his heel and walked away. Payne afterwards averred that his words had gone hime, but on the other hand the Squire may well have been taken aback by his effrontery in uttering them.

The meeting was arranged for six o'clock at Wormwood Scrubs. Not having his own pistols with him, Osbaldeston had borrowed a pair from Sir St Vincent Cotton, the same man whom Bentinck had so gratuitously insulted in White's. Made

---

* Considering the amount of money he had himself won on Rush — at least to some extent at Osbaldeston's expense — this was a quite extraordinary statement for Payne to have made.

by the famous gunsmith John Manton of Dover Street, they were a beautiful pair but of rather large bore.

When the Squire entered his carriage to take him to the duelling-ground he found Mr Humphreys already there. Humphreys's conversation convinced him that his second was in a conspiracy to prevent him from killing Lord George. 'After his unjustifiable language to you', Humphreys said, 'it is impossible that he can try to shoot you, and indeed I have very good reason to know that he don't [*sic*] intend it. Under these circumstances it would amount to very nearly a case of murder if you killed him, and like shooting an unarmed man.'

Since Osbaldeston had been alerted by a friend that Humphreys was under an obligation to Lord George, and that this was the only reason he had consented to act, he took very little notice of these protestations. Just before they arrived Colonel Anson stopped his carriage and entered the Squire's to ask if they could use one of his pistols, since Lord George did not possess any himself. When Osbaldeston agreed he examined the weapons and commented on their large bore. 'It's as good for the goose as the gander,' Osbaldeston commented coolly.

Lord George was waiting for them dressed from head to foot in black, so as to present as small a target as possible to his adversary. When the distance — twelve paces — was measured out, the seconds took the pistols away to load and prime them. A man was ploughing on the other side of the hedge bordering the field in which they were. So as to attract as little attention as possible, Colonel Anson and Mr Humphreys sat in the ditch to attend to the pistols. According to what Humphreys later told Osbaldeston, Anson's hands were shaking so much that he could do nothing and Humphreys alone carried out this task. When it was completed they returned to the two parties and handed them the pistols. Anson then took charge.

The exact truth of what happened next will never be known, and much nonsense has been written about it including the statements that Lord George's shot went through Osbaldeston's mutton-chop whiskers (he hadn't any) and that Osbaldeston put his ball through Lord George's hat. There can, however, be little doubt about two things — the first that Colonel Anson, knowing their respective abilities as pistol shots and being determined to preserve Bentinck's life at all costs, took deliberate measures to confound Osbaldeston's aim, and, second, that Bentinck fired first.

Sir Theodore Cook, the distinguished editor of *The Field* and authority on Turf history, is disposed to accept Osbaldeston's own account of the matter and this is what the Squire says happened:

Colonel Anson approached him and said: 'I am to give the word, Ready, fire!'

When he said 'Ready!' Osbaldeston raised his hand and cocked his pistol. Anson immediately said: 'That won't do!' When Osbaldeston lowered his hand Anson walked a few paces away in a direction almost opposite to where Lord George was standing. Then, when he stopped, he called on Osbaldeston to look towards him, thus taking the Squire's eyes off his antagonist. Immediately he saw that he had caught Osbaldeston's attention and his glance Anson called out: 'Ready! Fire!' Lord George shot immediately and missed.

Osbaldeston now had his man at his mercy. He had all the time in the world and could kill him as he liked. Knowing this, he says that he felt his anger dissipate. Honour had been satisfied; vengeance would best be served by a contemptuous dismissal of his man. He fired wide. This all rings true. He was never a vindictive man and he had already spared one life — Gully's — in a duel. The moment he discharged his weapon, however, he realized that it had not been loaded.

The statement that his pistol had never been loaded has been disputed, notably by E. D. Cuming who wrote a commentary on Osbaldeston's memoirs. Cuming says it would be tantamount to accusing the seconds of attempted murder if they had loaded Bentinck's pistol and not Lord George's. This is of course true, but the correct explanation, almost certainly, is that they were so desperate to save Bentinck's life that they loaded neither weapon. Cuming attempts to dispose of this theory by saying that, if this were the case, why was Anson so nervous? But Anson's nerves were in disarray long before the loading, which was carried out by Humphreys alone. Cuming also adds that if he knew the pistols were not loaded why did Anson try to throw out Osbaldeston's aim? But it is highly probable that Anson was taking every possible precaution in case something went wrong, since he had not carried out the loading himself and was also attempting to give verisimilitude to the whole sorry affair. One thing, as Sir Theodore Cook says, is indisputable, and that is that neither man was touched and, he adds, 'A man who could hit an ace of diamonds at thirty paces was not likely to miss the commanding figure of his antagonist at twelve, had he really desired to kill him,' and, it may be added, had the pistols been loaded.

Seeing Bentinck standing unharmed Anson, no doubt from nervous relief, turned to Osbaldeston and said, both foolishly and tactlessly: 'Well, Squire, I did not think you were so bad a shot.'

'Perhaps on another occasion it may turn out differently,' the Squire growled back. 'The colonel', he goes on to say, 'then joined his friend, no doubt congratulating himself on having saved his lordship's skin.'

There, for the moment, the matter ended. But, as may be imagined, all fashionable London was a-buzz about it and when it came to the Duke's ears he was not best pleased with his son, despite the fact that Colonel Anson, ever the courtier, had written to him to say that Bentinck had 'acted in a manner above all praise, that can only raise him in the estimation of all who know him'.

Bentinck himself addressed a letter on the subject to his father. In its conscious self-justification it is typical of the man:

My dear Father,
    George Anson has kindly undertaken to write you an account of my affair with Osbaldeston. I do not expect you will do otherwise than condemn the folly and indiscretion in the first instance in telling the man the truth to his face; — but I trust you will at the same time think I was at least right in morality as well as in honour when once I had uttered a charge, which in my conscience I believe to be just, to adhere to it and firmly refuse to retract or to qualify it.

47

I hope there is no man who would be more ready or anxious to make fullest reparation and the most ample and humble apology, than I should be, where any honest man could pretend I had wronged or done injustice in the slightest degree to another; — but where I was well assured I had done neither wrong nor injustice but spoken out the truth, and nothing but the truth, I should have been ashamed of myself if I had been contented to purchase personal security by sacrificing the truth and denying the truth for any personal consideration.

The difficulty O found in getting any man to accompany him, and eventually declaring himself satisfied with one shot without any whisper of any apology or retraction from me are incontestible proofs of the justice of my accusation.

With respect to George Anson, I can never forget the real kindness, ability and earnestness with which he managed my part of the transaction, not fearing to identify himself with every charge I had made, whilst he left no stone unturned to induce Mr Humphrey to throw up his commission....

The Duke, however, did not quite see it in the same light as his son, and wrote back:

Dear George,

We must thank heaven you have not been hurt.

I certainly think that nothing but the most positive certainty that Mr O had been guilty of the robbery imputed to him, could excuse you from giving him satisfaction in the field for such expressions as you used to him. But I also think that nothing less could excuse the use of such language.

That certainty perhaps exists now which did not exist then — for if he had not been conscious of the justice of the charge he would hardly have been satisfied with the mode of exculpation, or when he had chosen it would have been satisfied so easily.

I had heard that you had used strong language, but not so strong as that which you did use to Mr O. — having heard it, I was sorry that I had allowed myself to be one of those who were added to the Stewards when they enquired into his conduct. I did not suspect any further consequences then. But I hope now that the event will at least have the good consequence of impressing upon you the necessity of attending to that good rule *'Animum rege qui nisi paret imperat.'*

I always admired the late Mr Sherbrooke, who was born with a bad temper but taught himself to keep it in subjection.

Ever dear George,
Yours affy,
SCOTT PORTLAND.

It has been widely said that some years later a reconciliation took place between the parties and that Lord George, on consideration, felt that his conduct had perhaps been too hasty and his words too severe. It was not in his nature to do so, and the 'reconciliation' may have been a ruse on Lord George's part to obtain something he badly wanted.

The Bibury Club was then at the height of its fame and exclusiveness. It was an association of amateur jockeys which held races confined to its members. Two black balls were sufficient to exclude a candidate. Osbaldeston was a member but Lord George was not, and he badly wanted to become one. When attending the meeting he had to put up at the local inn and not in the Club, which did not suit his pretensions at all. He therefore asked his then trainer, John Day, to find out, if he was proposed, whether the Squire would blackball him. Osbaldeston never bore malice and when the question was put to him he replied: 'Certainly not'. Lord George was therefore proposed and duly elected. As a *quid pro quo*, as it were, he put Osbaldeston up on one of his horses at the next meeting and afterwards invited him to inspect his stud. It was therefore widely believed that the hatchet had been buried. However, it is almost certain that Lord George had made use of Osbaldeston's known generosity of character to get elected to the Bibury Club, which had long been one of his ambitions, and that his feelings towards his former adversary had not changed. A little later he told John Kent, who was then training for him, that there was no man's money he more desired to win than Osbaldeston's unless it was that of his hated cousin George Greville, and when his John of Gaunt beat Osbaldeston's Sorella his normally impassive features 'showed every sign of extreme pleasure and jubilation'.

However, if, as seems likely on all the evidence, neither pistol was loaded for the duel, it is inconceivable that Lord George should have known of this beforehand for, with all his faults, he would never have betrayed himself into condoning such a subterfuge. Sir Theodore Cook's summing-up of the whole affair seems a sound one. 'Lord George', he wrote, 'had deliberately risked his life for what he considered to be the principles of honest betting on the Turf, *principles which he allowed no man except himself to interpret.*' [Author's italics.]

CHAPTER 3

Palmer the Poisoner

ON 12 MAY 1856 William Palmer, aged thirty-one, of Rugeley, surgeon, 'of superior degree of instruction' was indicted 'for having at Rugeley, County of Stafford, on 21st November 1855, feloniously, wilfully and with malice aforethought committed murder on the person of John Parsons Cook'. The facts which led up to one of the most famous criminal trials of the century, one which has given rise almost to a literature of its own, and to doubt and discussion ever since, were bizarre indeed.

William Palmer was a personable man — generous, amiable, of good presence and considerable ability in his chosen profession. He was also, as events were to show, possessed of an unshakeable nerve, steadiness under stress and cool courage in adverse circumstances. But, to use an expression he would probably have employed himself, the blood was bad, for he came of tainted stock.

Palmer's maternal grandfather, a man named Bentley, had begun life as pimp to a notorious brothel-keeper known as Peg Taff of Micklover. One of his tasks was to bank the lady's takings every week. Since she was illiterate and had no means of checking his dealings with the bank, he placed the money in his own name. When it had reached a sum he thought sufficient for his needs he decamped, taking the savings with him and leaving the lady stranded.

Bentley now set himself up in business. He prospered and

became respectable, married a lady of some property and settled down to the life of a substantial merchant in the village of Aston Hayes. There his daughter Sarah, Palmer's mother, was born. As she grew up Sarah acquired a reputation in the locality for being fast and flighty and over-fond of men.

Joseph Palmer, William's father, was a sawyer, and stated in contemporary accounts to be 'a coarse, vulgar fellow'. He was friendly with Hodson, the Marquess of Anglesey's steward, who was one of Sarah's suitors. Palmer became his rival in love, captured the lady's affections and married her. This did not interfere with their friendship; indeed it was widely held that they continued to share her favours and both Palmer himself and his elder brother William were said by some to have been sired by Hodson.

Palmer and Hodson evolved a system of double- or treble-marking the trees for sale in the Anglesea forests, thus swindling the estate out of a considerable sum of money. Later Palmer got to know the steward on the Bagot estate and repeated the process there. Soon he became a man of some property, trading as a timber merchant in Rugeley.

William Palmer, the third son and sixth child in a family of seven, was born on 21 October 1836 at Rugeley and brought up there. Just before his twelfth birthday his father dropped dead after his evening meal. He left a fortune of £70,000 and no will. Joseph, the eldest son, settled £7,000 on each of the children, leaving the residue with Sarah provided she did not marry again.

The elder Palmer had been a stern father and taskmaster but after his death the strings of parental authority were relaxed. Always inclined towards promiscuity, Sarah took lovers, many of whom were ludicrously younger than herself. She indulged and petted her children, but mostly they were allowed to go their own way unsupervised and unchecked.

It was not a healthy atmosphere in which to grow up, especially as Sarah, the eldest sister, early became a confirmed alcoholic as well as practising certain vices of which a contemporary chronicler declared: 'decency will not allow us even to allude to in print'. Walter, the brother next in age to William, was 'very rackety' and he, too, soon set out on a career of drink and debauchery which ultimately led to his death.

Rugeley was a racing and hunting centre. Horses and racing fascinated William from the first, and he always seems to have been an improvident and unlucky gambler. He was given a good schooling at Rugeley Grammar School and later was apprenticed to a wholesale chemist in Liverpool. Here most of his time and such money as he could lay hands upon was spent at Liverpool and Chester races, in female company 'of the lowest sort'. Throughout his life his tastes and habits outran his means, and soon his fingers were in his employer's till. Never short of ideas or ingenuity, he had thought out an almost undetectable system of extracting money from postal packets. So clever was it that it took months of intensive detective work by his employers and the Post Office authorities before he was found out and the deficiencies traced to him. Caught red-handed and charged with the crime, his nerve did not fail him. He refused to confess until extreme pressure was exerted and the threat of imminent imprisonment produced by his accusers. His mother saved him by repaying the stolen money.

He was next apprenticed to a surgeon at Tylecot near Rugeley. Here he swindled his master by putting such fees as he collected into his own pockets. On the proceeds he kept a mistress, whom he entertained lavishly at the local inns, went racing and gambling, and was ultimately dismissed for — it was alleged, though never proved — tearing up another apprentice's clothes and pouring acid over them in revenge for an imagined slight. If in fact he did do this he was acting out of character, for he was never a vindictive man. Despite his dissipations, too, he was well liked by his patients, who appreciated his kindliness and pleasant manner and his readiness to turn out for them at any time of the day and night.

Eventually he enrolled as a student at St Bartholomew's Hospital. Here he gave his expensive tastes full run, entertaining his friends to champagne breakfasts, keeping up with the swells in the supper-room at Evans's, the then fashionable sporting hostelry, racing, gambling, and becoming something of a figure

amongst the racing fraternity, who were branded by the respectable as 'flashy in dress, shallow in intellect and depraved in
morals'.

The other side of his character was, however, also in evidence.
He was considerate and helpful to those on whom he attended,
particularly to the poorer patients. He tried to assist them
financially when they were leaving hospital, sending the hat
round for them and contributing generously to such sub-
scriptions himself. In 1846, to the surprise of his family and
friends, and by dint of employing one of the best crammers of
the day — whom he omitted to pay — he qualified as a surgeon
and was entitled to style himself MRCS and 'William Palmer,
Esq., Surgeon'.

Returning to Rugeley, he set himself up in practice and the
following year married Anne Thornton, the illegitimate
daughter of a Colonel Brookes. Brookes lived with his servant,
Anne's mother; he was said to have money, but owing to the
liaison he was not received in polite society in Rugeley, and
there was insanity in his blood. His four brothers had all
committed suicide, as ultimately he did himself — some said
driven to it by his mistress's nagging about her thwarted social
ambitions. Whatever caused it, there is no doubt that the
mother was a termagant from whom her daughter was glad
to escape.

If he had been in any degree able to control his extravagances, Palmer would have prospered. He had enough knowledge of his chosen profession to get by; he had a good
appearance and an engaging manner and women, especially,
liked him. But the racecourse, horses, and above all gambling,
held him in thrall.

Once qualified, with some money coming in from the
practice, a small dowry from his wife — he is said to have
expected much more — and funds available from his ever-
indulgent mother, he was not content to go racing as a mere
spectator: he had to take a more active part.

At first he confined himself to breeding and horse-coping. He
bought land and stables just outside Rugeley and installed there
a stud-groom, his brood mares and the horses he bought with a

view to selling on. He had a good eye for a horse and was skilful in handling them. He was knowledgeable about breeding, too, and here again he might have prospered had it not been that, like many gamblers, he had no business sense at all. He bought too dear and, governed as he was, again like many gamblers, by whims and fancies, he sold too soon or too late and almost invariably too cheap. His financial failures drove him to frequent the racecourse more and more in an endeavour to recoup his losses. As a result he became known in Rugeley as 'the sporting surgeon'; there were rumours of inattention to the practice, and patients fell away.

Tales of his high-living, too, began to be put about. One in particular concerned a riotous party he gave on Derby Day at Epsom which ended in an upset coach on the journey home and 'a night of debauchery' in London. These stories gained strength and credence in the town and proved shocking to its staider elements. That was bad enough, but then much more sinister rumours dealing with other activities of the sporting doctor began to circulate, at first in whispers and then more openly.

A year after the marriage a son was born. He was followed in quick succession by three other sons and a daughter. Only the eldest survived infancy and all died in the same way — in convulsions. Palmer, not a discreet man, had often been heard to proclaim that large families did not justify the expense of their upbringing. It began to be openly alleged that he poisoned these children by smearing his finger with antimony, coating it in sugar and sticking it down their throats.

Not without cause an evil reputation began to grow up around him. In the space of a few years racing and gambling had become all but an obsession with him. To give himself more time for these pursuits he engaged a man called Benjamin Thirlby as an assistant and very soon Thirlby was in charge of virtually the whole of his practice. But these activities all cost money and, conducted on the scale to which Palmer was accustomed, large sums of it. As usual his gambling, too, was going badly. After a few years of marriage he was in perilous financial straits.

Believing that on the death of his mother-in-law his wife would inherit at least £12,000, he persuaded Anne Thornton Senior, much against her will and that of his wife, to come and live with them. Shortly after her arrival she was troubled by nausea and vomiting. These symptoms persisted and grew worse. Within a fortnight she was dead. She died raving and shrieking imprecations at Palmer as he stood watching by the bedside, her last lucid words being: 'Take that awful devil away!' Dr Bamford, aged eighty and doting, a friend of Palmer's who had brought him into the world, obligingly certified the cause of death as apoplexy.

The money inherited on his mother-in-law's death, though less than he had expected, helped Palmer over his pressing difficulties. However, shortly afterwards another suspicious death made his increasingly bad reputation even worse.

One of Palmer's racing acquaintances was a young man called Bladon, to whom he owed gambling debts amounting to, it was said, about £400. Together they went to Chester races. There Bladon was a winner and he agreed to return to Rugeley with Palmer — Palmer had told him that he could get him some shooting and that he would settle with him during his stay since he, too, had come out on top from the meeting.

Bladon agreed and was entertained in Palmer's usual lavish style. Brandy was now Palmer's favourite tipple and he had perfected the technique of draining his glass at one gulp, saying, not very convincingly, that this improved the flavour of the drink. But some of those who suspected him believed he did this to disguise the taste of the poison with which he had laced the drinks of people from whose deaths he expected to profit. During his stay Bladon drank drink for drink with him, and very soon he became ill with the usual symptoms of nausea and vomiting. At first Palmer treated him himself, then he called in the assistance of the obliging Dr Bamford. No news of Bladon's illness was sent to his wife. She knew nothing at all of it until an acquaintance of Bladon's, knowing he was staying with Palmer, called to give him what he had heard was a certainty for the following week's racing. So distressed was this acquaintance by

Bladon's appearance that he insisted on Mrs Bladon being told of the illness. Hurrying to his bedside, she found him delirious and at the point of death. Shortly afterwards he died without recognizing her. When she asked for his effects she found that they had been ransacked, there was no money at all amongst them, and his betting book was missing.

Bladon's other relatives and his employers wanted to put the matter in the hands of the police. His wife, poor woman, was distraught. She had received kindnessess at the hands of Mrs Palmer not only on this but on other occasions. She was unwilling to cause her further unhappiness and it is only fair to quote from a letter she wrote to a friend who was particularly active in his accusations:

> Now as regards the notions William and you seem to entertain of his brother's death, I entertained no such suspicions. I felt, and still feel, extremely obliged to Mrs Palmer for her kindness to me, which could not be greater if I had been a relative of her own. Consider how shocking it would appear, without some proof more than mere surmises, to accuse anyone of a foul crime, which your letter more than hints at. If your mind is not easy, go over yourself and make enquiries; but pause ere you do anything to render Mrs Palmer so uneasy as so dreadful a suspicion must make her. That Mr Palmer has acted unjustly in money matters I have good reason to believe....

The investigation was abandoned and the matter dropped. But rumour proliferated for Palmer had profited, it was said, to the tune of £1,000 by his friend's death, since he had pocketed all the ready money in his effects and the debt due from Palmer to him was never paid.

Then an uncle of Palmer's, 'Beau' Bentley, died after drinking copious draughts of brandy with him and adopting his method of 'gulping'. Another racing acquaintance, a man called Bly, fell ill of the same symptoms — nausea and vomiting — which had characterised the other victims, after accompanying him to Leicester races and winning a sum of money from him. When Bly was dying he told his wife to apply to Palmer for this money, £800, if he died. After his death the wife sought out Palmer and demanded the money. The bland reply was that her husband must have been suffering from death-bed delusions since in fact the money was owed not by Palmer but to him — however in view of the sad circumstances of her husband's death he would magnanimously waive any claim to it.

Nothing further came of this matter either and Palmer went on his way ignoring the constant wagging of tongues. Soon these nefarious acts, combined with a lucky run of winners, enabled him to do what he had always wanted and become an owner. His colours — 'all yellow' — were registered and he sent his horses to be trained at nearby Hednesford by Will Saunders, a well-known and well-liked trainer in the district.

On the Turf, as an owner, Palmer was popular. He was quietly dressed and unassuming, and he ran his horses openly and straight. The famous John Osborne of Ashgill found him 'a nice agreeable man to talk to'. He had a nerve of iron and accepted both defeat and victory just as they came, without change of countenance or demeanour. Some of the best jockeys of the day rode for him. Among them George Fordham, to whom, as a very young man, he sent a cheque for £27 'for riding Lurley at Shrewsbury and Wolverhampton and expenses', the great Nat Flatman, who was just pipped for second place in a two-year-old race at Brighton on Rip Van Winkle — the only horse of Palmer's own breeding, oddly enough, ever to run in his colours — W. Sharpe and Charley Marlow, the Cock of the North.

After his death Palmer was accused of stopping his horses by administrations of strychnine, but this is almost certainly untrue because he always wanted to win. There was, however, a strong suspicion that he was instrumental in getting at the favourite in the Marquess of Anglesey's Plate at the Rugeley October meeting in 1853. Palmer ran his own mare, Doubt, in that race. The night before someone pushed a carrot impregnated with arsenic into the favourite's stable at the Crown Inn. As a result the favourite did not run and later died from the effects of the poison. Doubt won at a long price and Palmer backed her. This horse had already figured earlier that year in another incident which did nothing to lessen Palmer's dreadful and growing reputation and which almost ended in tragedy.

Two of the biggest and most reputable bookmakers of the day were George Hodgman and Frederick Swindell, who were also close friends. Doubt was entered in the Wolverhampton Handicap. Swindell was acquainted with Palmer who frequently betted with him. Hodgman and Swindell would usually go to Wolverhampton together but on this occasion Hodgman could not travel, and Swindell told him he was going up with Palmer. Knowing Palmer's reputation, Hodgman warned his friend to be careful.

'Thanks,' Swindell replied. 'But I shall be all right. Bye the bye he says he has a good thing in Doubt for the handicap. I've put him £500 on at sevens and I've got £250 on myself.'

The important thing to note about that statement is that the bet, £3,500—£500, was made in Swindell's name and, as Hodgman later pointed out, if Swindell died before settling-day and Doubt lost, the bet would be void.

Palmer and Swindell stayed in Hodgman's rooms in the Swan at Wolverhampton, and on the evening they arrived Palmer persuaded Swindell to try his method of 'gulping' brandy. A fair amount was consumed in this way and the next day Swindell was so ill that he could not attend the races. The handicap was the big betting race of the day. There were nine starters and Doubt was largely ignored in the market. The mare was, as Hodgman said — though Swindell did not know it — quite literally running for the bookmaker's life. In the end she did it — just — by half a length.

It was now in Palmer's interest to save the life he had put in peril and to apply the antidote. Hurrying back from the track he poured hot soup into his intended victim, chafed his legs in front of a hot fire and administered other remedies. Swindell recovered but remained shaky for some little time afterwards. It is a tribute to the personal charm Palmer exercised over his friends and acquaintances that Swindell bore no malice and later tried to persuade the prosecuting counsel at Palmer's murder trial, Cockburn, to 'be easy with him'.

Swindell's life was saved but Palmer's list of murders was far from finished. He was always driven on by his gambling losses and his need for money. Twice he was posted as a defaulter at Tattersall's. But through it all he somehow managed to keep up appearances and to retain his popularity both on the racecourse and in the district. Amongst the few patients he retained were the parents of John Porter, the great trainer, who lived at Rugeley. They remembered him as being 'accounted very clever in his profession, and with his cheery, companionable manner, popular with both patients and friends'. But they also knew of his financial troubles and had seen a letter from Palmer to a friend which demonstrated the financial straits to which he was reduced from time to time. 'Will you please', Palmer wrote, 'go with the bearer to Mr —— and ask him to send me £5 if he has it. If not, ask him to borrow it. . . or else I am sure I must go to gaol. God bless you! I must have the £5 somehow or other.'

It may well have been this £5 which was all he could afford to wager when his mare, Goldfinder, won the Tradesmen's Plate at the Chester May meeting. Carrying 7st 6lb, she won at 30—1 because Palmer could find neither the cash nor the credit to back her. She did, however, net him the comfortable stake of £2,770 which, temporarily at least, kept his creditors at bay.

It was Goldfinder, too, which brought off his greatest coup by winning the Chester Cup. There were twenty-nine starters and the winning verdict was 'half a neck'. In fact in the opinion of many it should have been a dead heat with the runner-up, Talfourd. Palmer cleared £12,000 in bets in addition to the handsome stake. Since the whole of Rugeley to a man was on the mare he was the most popular person in the district and the hero of the hour.

But the money went through his fingers like quicksilver. Goldfinder let him down in the Queen's Plate at Shrewsbury. Morning Star won the Cleveland Cup at Wolverhampton and again at Rugeley but was unplaced when heavily backed in all his other starts.

As Palmer's debts grew so did his ambitions. He determined

to step up the class of his horses and take a tilt at the classics. In the following year he purchased two potentially top-class horses in Nettle and The Chicken. Nettle, a Sweetmeat filly, had won the Gimcrack Stakes and was fancied for the Oaks. Each of these horses cost him £2,000 and he raised the money by forging acceptances on bills in his mother's name. The bills were discounted by Mr Padgwick, a well-known and ruthless racing money-lender of the time.

Even before he plunged into the crime of forgery Palmer was under severe financial pressure, and indeed it was this which drove him into the last desperate gamble of going for a big win with Nettle in the Oaks. Money had to be found somewhere, however, to stave off his creditors' demands and to keep his string going until that race came round.

Early in the year he had managed to insure his wife's life for £14,000 though the premium, £760, was far beyond his means to pay. In September she caught a chill while returning from a concert in Liverpool. When she reached home she took to her bed and Palmer treated her. Soon afterwards the familiar symptoms of nausea and vomiting developed. By the end of the week she was dead. Ben Thirlby, Palmer's partner, the obliging Dr Bamford, and a Dr Knight who was called in towards the end and who was also over eighty, all signed the death certificate saying she had died from 'English cholera'. On the strength of this certificate the insurance company paid up and Palmer was once more temporarily in funds.

He noted in his diary that he was 'grief-stricken' at the death of his 'poor dear Annie. I shall not long stop after her!' and at the funeral he appeared distraught. But on the night she died he seduced her maid, Elizabeth Tharm, to whom an illegitimate child was born nine months later.

About this time Palmer met and made friends with a young man called John Parsons Cook. They were seen constantly on the racecourse together and Cook most probably looked to Palmer as the more experienced racing man for advice and assistance in his betting and purchase of horses. In time, Cook acquired two useful animals in Polestar and Sirius.

Cook had originally been articled to a solicitor, but he had never cared for the law and had grown bored. His spirit yearned for a more exciting way of life, and on inheriting £13,000 he took to the Turf. Physically he was not strong. Once on the Turf he threw in his lot with the fast men of the day and the dissipations which he enjoyed in their company damaged an already weak constitution. His medical advisers and friends implored him to abandon the life he was leading but, like Palmer, he was obsessed by horses and racing, and he refused. Despite his weak constitution he was active enough and during the winter months he hunted and shot. At the trial it was suggested that he was suffering from syphilis or had suffered from it. This was never proved but there is little doubt that he, at least, believed he had contracted the disease and was dosing himself with mercury pills.

Palmer's insurance money disappeared very quickly — much of it to Mr Padgwick, who was not inclined to wait for payment — and once again he had to look around for some means of financing his horses in the coming year. He was sure the filly, Nettle, would win him the Oaks. If he could find the money to plunge on her, she would, he was convinced, free him from his financial troubles. His brother Walter was an incorrigible alcoholic, and Palmer now set about trying to insure his life. The figure he fixed on was no less than £82,000. He tried six different companies and all refused him. One doctor wrote in his report to the company: 'He insured his wife's life for many thousands and after the first payment she died. BE CAUTIOUS.' In the end Palmer could only obtain a policy worth £14,000 with the Prince of Wales — the same company, oddly enough, that had insured his wife's life and paid up.

In the meantime the flat racing season opened. Although she did not have a preliminary race before the Oaks, Nettle's preparation went according to plan and she was strongly fancied. Palmer backed her with every penny he could lay hands on and every shilling of credit he could obtain. Were she to win, he was confident that he could settle with his creditors once and for all. He needed to, for renewals of the bills with his mother's forged acceptances on them were becoming due. In May, shortly before the Oaks was due to be run, he had to obtain Cook's acceptance on a bill for £190 in order to stave off a writ. About this time, too, he and Cook shared a partnership in a mare called Pereine. A friendly disagreement arose between them about running her and finally they tossed a coin to decide who should own her outright. Palmer won, the mare proved to be useless, and he remarked that he had won a loss. As well as all this his brother Walter, though his alcoholism was becoming worse and he was now drinking almost three bottles of spirits a day and eating nothing, steadfastly refused to die.

Despite these pressures on him Palmer continued to look after his racing affairs with promptness and efficiency. He engaged Charles Marlow to ride Nettle in the Oaks and on 17 May he despatched a letter written in 'a bold, peremptory hand' to Henry Dorling, clerk of the course at Epsom:

> Dear Sir,
>   Be good enough to enter in the Craven Stakes at Epsom my br. c. The Chicken, 3 years old. I have enclosed you a cheque for his Stake and will pay you your fee when I come to Epsom, and I am dear Sir,
> Yours truly
Wm PALMER.
> PS I have sent Messrs Weatherby a cheque for my mare's Stake (Nettle) for the Oaks. WP

This letter was bordered by a black mourning band half an inch thick as a tribute to the bereavement he had suffered by the recent death of his 'poor dear Annie'.

On Friday 25 May, accompanied by Cook, he attended the Epsom meeting for the running of the Oaks. Cook and he lunched on chicken and champagne in their carriage. Then he strolled across, betting-book in hand, to watch the racing. As usual he was faultlessly turned out. His *sangfroid* was perfect as he greeted friends and acquaintances. No one could have guessed that his whole future depended on the running of his filly during the next few hours. It was said afterwards that he stood to win £16,000 on only two of the many bets he struck that afternoon. Nettle started favourite at 2—1 in a field of eleven.

Immediately the flag dropped Palmer's filly shot to the front —
and bolted. She fell over the chains near where the new mile
winning-post was then situated, ruined Palmer's hopes and
finances forever, and broke Charles Marlow's leg.

Palmer's demeanour did not change. 'What's that now in
front?' was his only comment on observing the disaster. When
Henry Dorling, meeting him after the race, commiserated with
him on his bad luck, Palmer drawled in reply: 'Yes it is rather a
bore, isn't it?' as if he had not a care in the world.

Charles Marlow's remark made in the hearing of Fred
Hodgman as they carried him in on an improvized stretcher was
rather more pointed. 'It serves me right,' he told a sympathizer.
'What business had I to ride a damned poisoner's horse!'

Palmer carried on running his horses as if nothing had
happened. But the pressures increased daily. Walter, despite the
fact that he was now all but permanently senseless with drink,
was still alive. The temptation to make sure of that £14,000 life
insurance money grew more and more alluring. Although
Walter was at least nominally under the care of another doctor
Palmer decided to attend him himself. On his visits he put his
horse up at the Junction Hotel in Stafford near where Walter
lived in Castle Terrace. The day before Walter's death the
landlord of the hotel came on Palmer in the yard dropping a
substance 'very carefully' from one bottle to another. In answer
to the landlord's enquiry as to his brother's health Palmer
replied: 'He's very ill, very low. I'm going to see him to take him
something more stimulating.'

The following day Palmer had two horses, Lurley and
Morning Star, running at Ludlow. He did not go to the meeting
himself but attended Walter instead. At mid-day Walter was
'seized with an attack of apoplexy' and died soon after. His
brother's death did not prevent Palmer wiring a friend on the
course to 'Lay £50 on Lurley for the Ludlow Stakes whatever
the price.' Immediately after the race had been run this was
followed by another telegram to the clerk of the course: 'Pray,
Mr Fraill, inform me who won the Ludlow Stakes.' In fact
Lurley was beaten and Morning Star won the Welter Cup
unbacked, all of which made Palmer's situation even worse. A

further catastrophe followed when the Prince of Wales insurance company, alerted by Walter's own doctor, refused to pay over the insurance money and, what was more, employed two private detectives to investigate the circumstances of his death. When the detectives came to interview Palmer they found him quite undisturbed by their visit and calmly consuming a meal of steak and kidney pie. On disclosing their suspicions to him he continued his meal with undiminished appetite, remarking to them as he did so that they must proceed as they had been instructed and that he was sure 'it was all very right and proper'.

But in fact all was very far from being very right and proper with Palmer. He had just previously persuaded Cook to assign two of his best horses, Polestar and Sirius, to Pratt, a money-lending solicitor and Padgwick's agent in London, as collateral for an advance of £500. The cheque was made payable to Cook. Palmer forged his friend's name on the endorsement and pocketed the £500. This sum could, however, only be a temporary panacea. Palmer tried to stave off the inevitable by taking out a life insurance policy on George Bates, a groom-gardener whom he employed from time to time, representing him in the proposal as 'a gentleman of independent means with a choice cellar and an independent income'. The insurance company, now deeply suspicious about all dealings with Palmer, sent down an investigator who found this gentleman 'of independent means' hoeing turnips! The risk was declined. By now the crash could only be just around the corner and in November it came.

The Attorney General's statement of Palmer's pecuniary situation at that time in his opening address at the trial is worth quoting in full:

In the month of November the account stood as follows. There were in Mr Pratt's hands a bill due on the 25th of October for two thousand pounds; another due on the 27th of October for two thousand pounds; two bills making together one thousand five hundred pounds, due on the 9th of November; a bill, due on the 10th of December for one thousand pounds; one on the fifth of January for two thousand pounds; one on the 18th of January for two thousand pounds; making in the whole £12,500. In July, it seems, Palmer contrived to pay one thousand pounds; thus in the month of November bills amounting to £11,500 remained due, and every one of them bore the forged acceptance of the prisoner's mother! You will therefore understand the pressure which necessarily arose upon him, the pressure of enormous liabilities which he had not a shilling in the world to meet, and a still greater pressure arising from the knowledge that, as soon as his mother should be resorted to for payment, the fact of his having committed these forgeries would at once become manifest and bring on him the penalties which the law exacts.

The week before the Shrewsbury races to which the Attorney General referred, and which were to set in train the sequence of events that led Palmer to the scaffold, he had been racing with Cook at Worcester. Cook had had a good day, clearing about £800 which he still had on him when he and Palmer travelled to Shrewsbury for the autumn meeting. Palmer, too, had won money at Worcester, but it had all gone in a desperate effort to stave off Pratt, to whom he had written: 'I will send you £250 from Worcester on Tuesday as arranged. For goodness sake do not think of writs; only let me know that such steps are going to be taken and I will get you the money even if I have to pay £1,000 for it; only give me a fair chance, and you shall be paid the whole of the money.' As a result of sending on the £250 Palmer had no ready money at all and had to borrow £25 to go to Shrewsbury with Cook.

Polestar, Cook's horse that had been pledged by way of security for the £500 on which Palmer had forged his signature, was entered for the Shrewsbury Handicap and won it by a neck, starting favourite in a field of twenty-two. The following day he won again, a sweepstake of 25 sovereigns, beating a solitary opponent over two miles with odds of 4—1 laid on him. Polestar, incidentally, must have been rather more than useful. He won seven races that year out of fifteen starts. Well might Palmer say, as he did when he was desperately trying to save something out of the débâcle: 'I must have Polestar!'

Cook, naturally enough, was delighted and excited by his

horse's success. He had plunged on him in the handicap partly in cash and partly on commission. His betting-book showed his winnings at £1,668 1s which, together with the stakes of £381 19s after deductions, gave him a profit on the races of just over £2,000, a substantial sum in those days.

On 14 November Cook entertained his friends, including Palmer, to dinner in the Raven Arms where they consumed a quantity of 'provincial champagne'. As was their custom when racing together, the two men had separate bedrooms but shared a sitting-room. The following evening, before they settled down to drink brandy and discuss the day's racing, Palmer had a visitor. This was a Mrs Ann Brooks, a racing woman of a type then practically unknown. She was married to a prominent Manchester businessman, but the union seems to have been one of convenience only, for Mrs Brooks went her own way. She betted heavily for herself and for others, both on commission and in cash. In addition she acted as unofficial agent for a coterie of jockeys, arranging their rides and looking after their finances, which most of them were hopelessly unqualified to manage for themselves. As a result of this she was brought into association with touts and hangers-on of all sorts and from them gleaned knowledge, some of it useful and much of it rubbish, about runners and their prospects at the local meetings.

Palmer had met Mrs Brooks in the street the previous afternoon; he wanted to know if she could find out anything about a horse called Lord Alfred who was in the same race as The Chicken and whom Palmer regarded as his principal danger. 'Be sure to call if you hear anything,' Palmer said to her.

About ten o'clock that evening she did call to see him at the Raven Inn. She found him in an upstairs passage at a table outside the sitting-room he shared with Cook, mixing 'a pale liquid' in a tumbler. As she watched he held the glass up to the light and examined the mixture carefully. He then went into his own room, emerging a few minutes later with a glass in his hand, and entered the sitting-room. While this was going on he had a desultory conversation with Mrs Brooks about the weather and the going, during which Palmer said he thought the ground was softening up which should suit The Chicken admirably. He then asked her if she would care for something to drink herself and she told him she would take a glass of brandy and water, and when he came out from the sitting-room he brought it. 'The glass was like the one I had seen in his hand before but the fluid was different,' she said. As she drank it they discussed the next day's racing and Mrs Brooks warned him that Lord Alfred was fancied. Palmer nevertheless repeated his remark about the going, said that he would still back The Chicken and advised her to do so as well. She suffered no ill effects from the brandy and water he had given her.

Shortly after Mrs Brooks left, a man called Ishmael Fisher, a friend of both Palmer and Cook who frequently settled for Cook, went into their sitting-room and found them drinking and chatting together. Cook suggested in Fisher's presence that Palmer should have another drink. Palmer said he would not until Cook had finished the drink in front of him. Thereupon Cook lifted his glass and drained it by 'the Palmer method' of gulping it down. Immediately he said: 'There is something in it. It burns my throat dreadfully.'

There was a drop or two left in the glass which Palmer took up and examined. He sipped the drop, tasted it and put down the glass. 'There is nothing in it,' he said. He then offered the glass to Fisher and a man called Read who had just come in. Since it was now quite empty they could pass no comment on its contents.

A little later Cook left the room. He returned after about ten minutes and asked Fisher to accompany him to his own room. There he made sure the door was shut and then, turning to Fisher, told him he had just been very sick. 'That damned Palmer has dosed me,' he said. He then gave Fisher all the ready money he had with him, amounting to about £800 in notes, and was promptly, in Fisher's presence, violently sick again. The vomiting went on for such a long time that Fisher called in an outside doctor, who examined Cook and left some medicine which Fisher gave to him and which seemed to control the vomiting.

Next morning Palmer told Fisher that when he had seen Cook earlier Cook had suggested that his drink of the night before had been doctored. 'I never play such tricks with people,'

Palmer said. 'I tell you what it was; he was damned drunk.'

Although Cook still complained of being very ill, he accompanied Palmer and Fisher to the races and saw The Chicken handsomely beaten by Lord Alfred. This did not make Palmer's financial position any better since he had put all he had on The Chicken. Cook, however, remained a substantial winner over the three days of the meeting. Moreover his suspicions of Palmer had either vanished or been blandished away by Palmer's charm, for he reclaimed his £800 from Fisher and arranged to return to Rugeley with Palmer. Once there he took up residence at the Talbot Arms, opposite Palmer's house.

Very soon he was taken ill again. His symptoms were the all too familiar ones of vomiting and nausea. Palmer was indefatigable, personally supervising not only his medicine but his diet, sending over bowls of broth cooked in his own house. As a result Cook became worse. The maid who took the broth over to him thought it looked and smelt so succulent that she yielded to the temptation of tasting it and was promptly sick herself.

Palmer then took the precaution of calling in the elderly Dr Bamford. The explanation of Cook's illness which Palmer gave to him was that Cook had over-indulged himself the night before. Bamford accepted this diagnosis without making much effort to confirm or contradict it. The symptoms, however, did not disappear and the patient became worse.

Monday was settling-day. Padgwick had threatened to serve the writs on foot of the forged acceptances on both Palmer and his mother unless he was paid. A sentence for forgery in those days meant deportation, so Palmer was now in deadly peril. On Monday morning he presented himself in London armed with a piece of paper which he said contained a list of Cook's winnings and an authority to collect them. Somehow he persuaded the various holders of Cook's money to act on this authority and, by a series of intricate and involved transactions, he succeeded in staving off for the moment any further action by those who were pressing him — especially Padgwick and his agent, Pratt. Padgwick however was by no means satisfied and urged on Palmer the necessity of making further substantial remittances. The matter, he said, 'must not be allowed to go to sleep'.

Palmer returned to Rugeley and immediately went to a surgeon's assistant whom he knew and obtained three grains of strychnine. From there he went to Cook's sick-bed. Cook had been better during the day, while Palmer was away in London, but that night he awoke in agony, semi-delirious and screaming 'Murder! Murder!' Palmer was sent for. He prescribed an opiate and the pain and delirium both subsided.

The next morning he was in the local chemist's shop ordering two drachms of prussic acid when, by coincidence, Newton, the same young man from whom he had received the strychnine pills the day before, walked in. On seeing him Palmer said he had something of importance to communicate to him, placed his hand on his shoulder and walked him outside the shop. It proved to be a very minor matter. While they were talking a mutual acquaintance came along and engaged Newton in conversation. Palmer returned to the shop and told the assistant to give him six grains of strychnine and some of Baily's liquor of opium.

Palmer then went back to his own house where he met a friend by arrangement. The friend thought that he had been asked round to receive settlement of a debt. Instead Palmer requested him to write out a cheque to be signed — he alleged — by Cook on Weatherby's for £350 in his, Palmer's favour. This, Palmer said, was his share of the stakes won by Polestar. 'Poor Cook is too ill to write it himself,' he said and went on to make the extraordinary statement: 'Messrs Weatherby might know my handwriting.' In the event, Weatherby's refused to pay the cheque, at first on the grounds that the clerk of the course had not forwarded the stakes and then, on further investigation, because the stakes had already been paid out to Cook on the course. The cheque was returned and never afterwards found or produced, a fact which the prosecution at the trial were not slow to allege pointed unequivocally to Palmer having forged its signature.

Palmer then resumed his attendance on Cook whose condition steadily worsened. As a result of this, Palmer said, he decided to call in one William Henry Jones, a doctor and close friend of Cook's with whom Cook stayed on and off. When Jones came he could find no symptoms of the biliousness or diarrhoea which Palmer had described to him. Later Palmer, Jones and Bamford had a joint consultation as to the treatment to be prescribed, and Palmer insisting in Cook's hearing on continuing the pills he had prescribed the night before. Cook immediately protested from his sick-bed that he would have no more pills since he blamed them for his attack during the previous night.

Desperation must now have been driving Palmer very hard indeed. First he induced Bamford to make up morphine pills to enable Cook to sleep. These he took away with him, having first made sure that their box bore Bamford's instructions in Bamford's hand. Later that night he went into Cook's room, showed the box of pills to Jones and at the same time commented on the clarity of Bamford's handwriting for a man of his years. Then, with some little difficulty, he persuaded Cook to take the pills. Cook vomited, but did not bring up the pills.

Jones was now sleeping in Cook's room, and after he had dined he returned to the bed he had had made up for him there. Cook seemed drowsy and hardly spoke. No sooner had Jones undressed, however, than Cook suddenly shouted that he was going to be sick, that he felt terribly ill and that a doctor should be fetched. A maid ran across the road for Palmer who found Cook gasping, screaming and in convulsions.

The patient implored Palmer to give him something to relieve his agony. Palmer gave him two pills saying that they contained ammonia and would help to ease his distress. With some difficulty Cook swallowed them. Almost immediately he vomited again. The convulsions continued and became worse. Fifteen minutes later Cook was dead. Jones, who was present during the entire death agony, was of the opinion that Cook had died of 'lockjaw tetanus'.

Having sent Jones to arrange the laying-out, Palmer stayed in the room with the body. When the laying-out women came they found him rifling Cook's effects. Later Palmer suggested to Jones that he should take them into his custody. Jones found no money at all beyond 'five sovereigns and five shillings', nor were there any letters, records or racing accounts. Most important of all, Cook's betting-book was missing. 'Where is the betting-book?' Jones asked Palmer.

'It is sure to be found somewhere,' was Palmer's reply. 'But it is of no use to anyone. All bets are void.' Palmer went on to say that Cook owed between £3,000 and £4,000, that he was responsible for it, and if Cook's friends did not pay up 'all my horses will be seized'. This was of course pure fiction and yet another desperate effort to obtain some ready cash.

The next morning John Porter, who was on holiday with his parents, was riding past Palmer's surgery when Palmer called to him. He asked Porter to take a note to Saunders telling him that Cook was dead. Porter did so and on returning home told his father what had happened. Porter's father remarked that it was very strange that so many people — thirteen to his knowledge — with whom Palmer had had dealings had died suddenly, and he added: 'There will be more about this, you will see.'

His forecast was correct. Jones informed William Stephens, Cook's stepfather, who came to Rugeley armed with his stepson's will. His suspicions were aroused by the absence of the betting-book, the general circumstances surrounding his stepson's death, and the rumours which were rife in the town. He demanded a post-mortem. Palmer's comment was: 'The poor fellow was full of disease; his throat was diseased and he had syphilis.'

Post-mortems were carried out but with singular inefficiency. No trace of strychnine was found, but there was some evidence of antimony, a poison which can cause vomiting and nausea. The circumstantial evidence connecting Palmer with Cook's death was, however, compelling and he did not help his own case by a clumsy attempt to interfere with the specimens from Cook's body when they were being brought to the pathologist for examination, and by offering the coroner a bribe of 'nice pheasants and a good hare', accompanied by a £5 note and a letter suggesting that the verdict should be: 'Died of natural causes and thus end it.'

On Saturday the fifteenth the coroner's jury brought in a verdict of wilful murder against Palmer and he was committed to Stafford Gaol. From now on even Palmer's resilience and ingenuity which had so far enabled him to escape the consequences of his crimes could not protect him.

Pratt, acting for Padgwick, had already issued proceedings on foot of the forged acceptances; shortly after Palmer's committal and arrest a creditor in Birmingham secured an order for sale of his personal belongings arising out of default on a bill for the substantial sum of £10,400. The cellar, according to the catalogue, yielded up 222 gallons of ale, 67 dozen of port and 43 gallons of spirits. In the dining-room were 'Two valuable oil-paintings: "Charles Marlow, the jockey, with Nettle", and "Goldfinder, winner of the Queen's Plate at Shrewsbury".' More relevant to the charge against Palmer, however, was a box containing fishing tackle 'and some pills' which was also offered for sale. Although the suggestion was made that these might well have been Dr Bamford's morphine pills for which Palmer had substituted his own containing strychnine, none of the authorities considered it worthwhile to have these pills impounded and examined.

In January the whole of Palmer's stud was sold at Tattersall's to defray his expenses. Doubt, who had so nearly brought about Fred Swindell's end, went to Mr Blenkiron for 81 guineas; Mr Padgwick bought a yearling colt and filly by Touchstone, paying 230 guineas for the colt and 250 for the filly. He sent them to be trained by Goater at Findon and both proved useless, which no doubt would have pleased Palmer had he known of it. Extraordinarily enough Major Grove, on behalf of the Prince Consort whom one would not have expected to care to associate his name in any way with such a sale, paid 230 guineas for Trickstress and went on to be the under-bidder for Nettle, one of the stars of the stable. She, however, was knocked down to Mr Popham for 230 guineas. The Chicken made the top price of 800 guineas and the aggregate was £3,906, no inconsiderable price for a small stud in those days.

The press was much less inhibited then than now in commenting upon matters which were *sub judice*, and all the public prints declared Palmer guilty and convicted long before the trial began. Local opinion was so strongly incensed against him that the defence applied to have the trial transferred from

Stafford to the Old Bailey. The application was granted, but since this had never happened before in a murder trial a special Act of Parliament had to be passed.

The authorities considered the trial so important and so complex that no fewer than three judges, Lord Campbell, the Lord Chief Justice, Mr Baron Alderson and Mr Justice Cresswell, were assigned to hear it. The Attorney General, Sir Alexander Cockburn, led for the prosecution, assisted by another silk and three juniors. Cockburn was an advocate of tremendous power and personality. He was an ambitious man, due for promotion to the Bench, and the successful outcome of a trial such as this meant much to him. He spent weeks marshalling the facts, preparing his case and, more significantly, mastering the details of the conflicting medical evidence likely to be offered, so that when he rose to open the case and went on to examine and cross-examine he had almost as much knowledge of strychnine poisoning, antimony, tetanus, and all the other varied theories to be put forward as did the medical experts themselves. 'Mark my words I am sure to hang him — sure,' he told Swindell, with whom he was friendly, when dining with him during the case.

It cannot be said that Palmer was as fortunate in his choice or, rather, his solicitor's choice, of his professional defenders as was the prosecution. On account of certain medical qualifications which he was thought to possess Mr Sergeant Wilkins was first approached as a leader. He agreed to act, but three weeks before the trial he sent back his brief and departed in haste to Dieppe pursued by duns. Then the ex-Attorney General, Sir Frederick Thesiger, was offered the brief and refused it. The final choice fell upon Mr Sergeant Shee, an Irishman and Member of Parliament for Kilkenny. Shee was an experienced and distinguished advocate but he was over-emotional, and he had only once before defended in a murder case. He was given little time to master the complexities of the case and the enormous difficulties presented by the defence. Shee was assisted by Grove KC and two juniors. One of these was Thomas Keneally who, brilliant though he was, was eccentric almost to the point of periodic insanity. He was later to gain both fame and notoriety as a result of his actions on behalf of the Tichborne claimant which ultimately led to his disbarment.

The case lasted twelve days and attracted enormous public interest. Prince Albert, the Prince Consort, had a report on the proceedings sent to him every day. Lord Campbell, the presiding judge, indulging in some hyperbole, described it as: 'The most memorable judicial proceedings of the last fifty years, engaging the attention of all Europe.'

Palmer himself was confident of an acquittal. Immediately after the arrest his nerve cracked for the first and only time. For six days he remained in bed, refusing either to eat or drink. When the governor informed him that if he continued he would be forcibly fed, Palmer recovered both his spirits and his composure. From that moment to the very end he remained master of his emotions, coolly assisting his legal advisers and displaying his firm belief in the successful outcome of the trial.

Despite the certainty in the minds of the public and of almost everyone connected with the matter that he had in fact killed Cook, he had some reasons for this belief for there were glaring weaknesses in the case for the Crown. 'I did not kill Cook by strychnia,' was the only comment he made when arrested. In these few words lay the whole kernel of the case, for Cockburn unhesitatingly told the jury that he would prove to them that Cook died from strychnine poisoning administered by Palmer. Yet the post-mortem examination had found no traces of strychnine in the organs. The evidence against Palmer was therefore purely circumstantial. The Crown had to show that the symptoms were so consistent with strychnine poisoning that they pointed irrefutably to it, that Palmer had the means and opportunity of administering it, and that he had strychnine in his possession. To counter this the defence maintained that the evidence was insufficient to sustain such a charge and that Cook's death was from natural causes, be they tetanus, 'syphilitic spasms', or what you will.

The trial in effect resolved itself into a battle, and at times a not very seemly one, between two sets of medical witnesses, each propounding and endeavouring to justify a differing explanation for Cook's death. There was, however, one very important

exception. Newton, the surgeon's assistant, was a vital prosecution witness concerning the sale of the three grains of
strychnine to Palmer on the Sunday night. At the trial he added
that he had had a conversation with Palmer in which Palmer
had asked him what dose of strychnine would be sufficient to kill
a dog. On being told by Newton 'a grain', he had enquired if it
would be found in the stomach after death. Newton said that it
would not, whereupon Palmer — according to Newton — said
'It's all right', and, as if speaking to himself, had snapped his
fingers.

Apart from the improbability of Palmer as an experienced
medical man asking a surgeon's assistant about the dosage and
effects of strychnine, Newton had said nothing at the inquest
about the sale of the three grains of strychnine nor about the
alleged conversation after it, nor did he disclose this evidence to
the Crown until three days before the trial opened. Yet Shee
deputed the cross-examination of this vital witness to his second
senior, Grove, who made no attempt to press Newton about his
withholding of this vital evidence. More important still, the
defence had not ascertained that Newton had a criminal record
— though not a very serious one — so that his credibility as a
witness of fact did not receive the close examination which it
required.

Throughout the long days of the trial Palmer's *sangfroid*
remained unruffled. He followed the evidence with the closest
attention, passing down to his counsel a stream of notes concerning the conduct of the case. One of these read: 'I wish there
was $2\frac{1}{2}$ grains of strychnine in old Campbell's acidulated
draught solely because I think he acts unfairly.' The comment
was not unjustified, for Campbell had been against him from
the first. His summing-up was hostile and he drew particular
attention to Newton's evidence so it may well be that this
distinctly doubtful testimony played a vital part in Palmer's
conviction.

There can be no doubt, too, that Cockburn's mastery of the
matter was far superior to Shee's, whose emotional outburst
during his speech for the defence declaring, in defiance of all the
canons of advocacy, his own belief in his client's innocence,

earned him a sharp rebuke from the judge and can have done him no good with the jury.

After being out for an hour and eighteen minutes the jury returned, bringing in a verdict of guilty. The judges put on their black caps and Lord Campbell, in a protracted and hectoring peroration to the prisoner, said amongst other things:

> William Palmer, after a long and impartial trial you have been convicted by a jury of your country of the crime of wilful murder. . . . The case is attended with such circumstances of aggravation that I do not dare touch upon them. Whether it is the first and only offence of this sort you have committed is known only to God and your conscience. . . . You must prepare to die. . . . We think that for the sake of example, the sentence ought to be executed in the county of Stafford. . . . I will not seek to harrow up your feelings with any enumeration of the circumstances of this foul murder . . . you will be taken to the place of execution and there be hanged by the neck until you are dead . . . and may the Lord have mercy on your soul. Amen!

Palmer received both the verdict and this dissertation without change of countenance. But as the Attorney General was about to leave the court he turned to one of the warders and, still looking at Cockburn, said, shaking his head: 'It was the riding that did it.'

Throughout the long days of waiting his nerve never failed him and, whatever his faults, he died as he had lived — game to the last. As he stepped on to the scaffold he tested the boards with his foot. 'Is this safe?' he asked the hangman. Those were his last words.

That Palmer had in fact murdered Cook there can be little doubt, but there will always be argument as to whether there was sufficient evidence to warrant conviction. Had a court of criminal appeal existed in those days there is at least a possibility that the sentence would have been quashed. After his execution 'a rascally barrister', to use Campbell's own words — generally believed to have been Keneally — directed to the Lord Chief

77

Justice a long and closely argued thesis setting out the incon-
sistencies and deficiencies of the case for the prosecution as
presented, and the iniquities of the summing-up.

There were two sequels to the whole affair which might well
have tickled Palmer's fancy had he known of them. The citizens
of Rugeley were so outraged by the notoriety brought upon
their town that they sent a deputation to the Prime Minister,
Palmerston, asking permission to change its name. 'By all
means, gentlemen,' was the cool reply, 'provided you name it
after me!' The name remained unchanged. More interesting
perhaps was the fact that the Cesarewitch the following year
was won in the 'commonest of canters' by The Chicken, who
had been renamed Vengeance. The runner-up was none other
than Polestar. Thus the poisoner's horse and that owned by his
victim were the first and second in one of the great betting
handicaps of the year after his execution.

CHAPTER 4

Admiral Rous and The Tarragona Affair

THE TARRAGONA AFFAIR involved no poisons, no pistols at dawn, and, compared with some of the more overtly sensational events that have happened in and around the Turf, seems almost anti-climactic. Its fascination lies in the fact that it shows a classic example of a trait of character that the racing world seems to bring out in all sorts of men, in this instance one who otherwise had a long and distinguished career on the Turf — blind prejudice to the point of obsession.

The following entry was made in the diary of an attaché to the British Embassy in Paris who subsequently became Ambassador in St Petersburg. 'As to the news the papers are crammed to a degree with that uncommonly nasty Jockey Club affair. In my opinion Admiral Rous seems to have behaved abominably and in any other age would have been horse-whipped.' The date of the entry was November 1862. In that year Admiral Rous was sixty-seven years of age. He had been a member of the Jockey Club for forty-one years; he had first served as a steward in 1838 and since 1846 had ruled unchallenged and supreme, 'a sort of perpetual president' in the councils of the Club. He was upright, incorruptible, and indefatigable in pursuit of what he thought to be malpractice, but by 1862 when that diary entry was written the wielding of absolute power had perhaps given him too strong a belief in his own infallibility. He was by then prone to take up positions from which neither advice nor persuasion could move him; he was despotic in implementing the decisions he made; he had been proved right so often and for so long that nothing could persuade him he might be in error. The difficulty in communicating with him was increased by his growing deafness. He also had a total abhorrence of anything shady in the way of betting. It was a combination of these factors that led to his undoing in the resounding Turf scandal that came to be known as the Tarragona affair.

It began innocently enough. A Colonel Burnaby of the Grenadier Guards owned a horse called Palm Oil in partnership with Captain the Hon. Randolph Stewart of the Black Watch, a brother of Lord Garlies. Neither of these gentlemen cared for the name Palm Oil and they decided to change it to Reindeer. Colonel Burnaby wrote down the new name as Raindeer. Stewart chided him, saying that the correct spelling was Reindeer, as in the modern usage. They both laughed over the difference and Burnaby bet his friend a fiver that his spelling was the correct one. At the time both were members of a racing house-party at Malmhead, a country house belonging to a mutual friend, Sir Lydstone Newman.

In the carriage going to Exeter races the same discussion about the spelling became general among the party. It was treated as a joke and bets were made. The subject again came up at dinner; more bets were struck and it was agreed to leave the decision to the dictionary. All this might have passed as the triviality it was had not a Mr Ten Broeck, an American who raced extensively in England at the time, been a member of the party. Ten Broeck offered to bet Stewart 100—1 on his interpretation of the correct spelling and Stewart took the bet. After dinner they searched for dictionaries and found that most of those in the house gave Stewart's usage as the correct one.

Ten Broeck, however, who did not take lightly to losing, on the racecourse or anywhere else, still insisted most forcibly that he was right so, for the sake of peace, Stewart offered to call the bet off. Still not satisfied, Ten Broeck next day called on Admiral Rous, gave him his version of the story and asked him to adjudicate.

As has been said, the one thing that Rous loathed above all other was any suggestion of shadiness in betting, especially between gentlemen. Ten Broeck appears to have suggested to him that he had been 'jockeyed' into making this bet by Burnaby and Stewart, who already knew the correct answer. With his usual impetuosity Rous accepted this suggestion as the truth and immediately decided to seek out and punish the wrong-doers. A day or so later, on the top of the Jockey Club stand at Doncaster, he accosted Stewart and demanded to know if he and Burnaby had made any bet on the spelling of the word Reindeer. On being informed by Stewart that he had, Rous said at the top of his voice, 'Then I give you up, you have not a leg to stand on!'; and, according to Stewart, 'throwing up his hands he rushed out of the stand without waiting for an answer'.

From that moment on, as he was to declare later, Rous 'utterly abhorred' Burnaby (although he had not seen him nor had he asked him to give his version of the affair) and he convinced himself that Burnaby and Stewart had acted in concert to swindle the other members of the house-party into making bets with them on something to which they already knew the answer. To cover what they had done he invented the term 'bubble bet'.

Even then things might not have got out of hand had not Burnaby and Arthur Annesley, a captain in his regiment, decided to run a match at the Newmarket meeting on 1 October. It was to be between Captain Annesley's Michel Grove and Colonel Burnaby's Tarragona. Michel Grove was to be ridden by the crack jockey, George Fordham, and Tarragona by Nightingall, who had managed and ridden Burnaby's horses for many years. The match duly took place and Michel Grove won easily by two lengths, having made all the running. There was some booing as the horses passed the post and almost immediately rumours began to fly that Tarragona had been pulled. A certain Mr Steele declared that he had heard Annesley and Burnaby concocting a false bet on the race so as to induce others to back Tarragona and lengthen the price on Michel Grove, which, he alleged, they had both backed.

The Duke of Beaufort, who had himself had a bet on the

outcome of the match, expressed himself ready to corroborate what Steele had said. On hearing this, Rous, without calling on either of the principals to explain the running and riding of their horses, said to himself, as he was later to admit, 'that it was most probable that a man who had made a bubble bet on one subject would do so on another'. He instructed C. Weatherby, the secretary to the Jockey Club, to inform Tattersall's committee that they should suspend payment of all bets on the match pending the result of an enquiry. He then dictated to Weatherby the letter he should send to the two principals, summoning them to the enquiry. This read:

> The Stewards of the Jockey Club propose, on Tuesday next at 10.30 a.m. to receive evidence respecting the extraordinary performance of Tarragona v. Michel Grove when you are required to attend.

The use of the words 'extraordinary performance' by the Admiral was at the least an indication that the case had been prejudged by him, and did not go un-noticed by society, the public or the press. By now the conduct of the Admiral over the two cases was being widely discussed at dinner tables. It had set society a-buzz, interviews were taking place between the various participants and letters were flying in all directions.

Before the hearing Annesley paid Rous a visit demanding to know exactly what he was being accused of, whereupon Rous rashly poured out to Annesley his story about the 'bubble bet' and made the statements about his abhorrence of Burnaby already mentioned. Annesley promptly conveyed these to Burnaby, who wrote in the strongest terms to Rous demanding an apology.

Rous was now discovering that he was not dealing with ordinary malefactors likely to lie down meekly under his thunderbolts. Both were officers in the Grenadier Guards. Burnaby had had a distinguished career, not only in action in the Crimea but in diplomatic posts abroad. Annesley was a member of White's and a brother of Lord Annesley, a member of the Jockey Club.

The next thing that happened was that the Earl of Portsmouth, one of the Jockey Club stewards, refused to sit on the enquiry on the grounds that he had been a member of the house-party where the original Reindeer bet had been made, which Rous was now trying to make part and parcel of the Tarragona affair. Rous immediately appointed Mr Caledon Alexander to act in his stead. This did little to reassure the participants, society or the public, since Mr Alexander was widely believed to have had a bet on the match himself. Feelings were now running so high, especially in society where it was widely held that Burnaby was being made a target for Rous's totally unreasonable suspicions and that Annesley had been dragged into the matter as an innocent victim, that Rous took another extraordinary step. He advised the stewards that since the matter might be 'difficult and painful' they should 'seek the assistance' of three other members of the Jockey Club and all six should sit as a special committee to hear this one case.

The stewards accepted Rous's advice, but the Admiral's choice of the three additional members did not reassure anyone anxious for the disinterested administration of justice. They were: Lord Stradbroke (his own elder brother), the Duke of Beaufort, who had had a bet on the match and who had already prejudged the issue by his outspoken opinions, and Lord Glasgow.

There is some reason to suppose that Rous was already beginning to feel that he could not sustain the accusations he had made, for at this juncture he made another of his rash statements to a friend. 'I must carry this matter through,' he said, 'or I shall never be able to show my face in Newmarket again.'

When the committee assembled under the presidency of Rous, Burnaby immediately protested about his taking and retaining the chair in view of the statements he had already made about the case and about Burnaby's character. His protest was brusquely over-ruled, though to do Rous credit he expressed his willingness to vacate the chair should the other members desire him to do so. Once confirmed in the chair Rous proceeded to act with almost unbelievable arrogance and partiality. His first act was to demand of Burnaby why, when he was accustomed to bet in thousands, he had only backed Tarragona for hundreds. Burnaby's reply that he had been badly hit the week before was received in stony silence, broken only by the Duke of Beaufort icily enquiring of him if he 'usually ran his horses straight?' Burnaby's indignant answer to this question had hardly been made when Rous flatly accused him of making a bubble bet on the Reindeer affair. Altogether it was a strange way to start a supposedly impartial enquiry.

The first witness to be called was Mr Steele, who had made the statement that had started the whole Tarragona affair. Under cross-examination by Annesley, however, he went back on his evidence and said he only 'thought' he heard the alleged conversation. 'I will not swear to it. I might have been mistaken,' he said. The Duke of Beaufort then said from his seat on the committee that he would corroborate Steele's original statement. Annesley immediately asked for permission to cross-examine the Duke. This was refused. The two accused then handed in their betting-books to prove the genuineness and accuracy of their statements concerning their bets.

Rous took the books and scrutinized them closely to see if he could detect any alteration. His naked eye having failed to do so, he then sent for a microscope under which he made a further examination. When this also failed to reveal anything he passed the books to the other members for their scrutiny. When they returned them to him saying that they also could not detect anything suspicious about the entries Rous was still not satisfied. He announced that he would send to the Bank of England for an expert 'skilled in detecting forgeries' who would carry out a further examination the following day.

That done, Rous turned his attention to the alleged stopping of Tarragona. The only evidence of this which could be produced was that of the starter, M'George, and his assistants. What weight this should have carried with the committee is debatable, especially since it was widely held that M'George's starts favoured the man who carried his money and he was under something of a cloud because of this. Further, he had been reported by Burnaby to the Hungerford stewards for misconduct at the start a week before the match in question. Burnaby's request to cross-examine M'George as to his personal animosity towards him was ruled out of order, but M'George may well have been shaken by it, for he contradicted himself twice during his evidence and finally admitted that 'they got off well'. His assistant revealed that he was eighty yards behind the flag when they started and thus not in a position to see anything. The flagman confessed that his opinion that Tarragona had been stopped stemmed from the fact that he had heard a friend say at the start: 'He is not going for the pieces,' or 'He has the strings on' — he was not sure which, but those were the expressions the friend used when he thought a certain horse was not off.

The following day Mr Arthur Crump, the expert from the Bank of England, arrived to examine the books. He testified that he could find no evidence whatsoever that the original entries had been tampered with or altered in any way. The committee then decided that, the matter being one 'of such unusual complexity', they would defer their decision until they met again at the Houghton meeting. They did, however, indicate to Tattersall's that all bets on the match should now be settled.

When the committee sat again at the Houghton meeting they issued a statement that they were 'of the opinion that it is not proved that Colonel Burnaby intended that Tarragona should be pulled or that he made a fictitious bet with Captain Annesley'. And then the fur really began to fly. It was, to say the least of it, a pusillanimous decision which satisfied nobody. By now the matter had achieved far more than parochial importance. The Jockey Club had published in full their account of the enquiry; the press had taken the matter up in a big way; both national and sporting papers devoted columns to it and letters arising out of both the Reindeer and Tarragona cases began to appear in the correspondence pages. Both letters and comment were almost universally condemnatory of Rous's conduct of the affair. Mr Harman Willes, who wrote under the pseudonym 'Argus' in *The Morning Post*, summed up the high feelings which were running against the Admiral.

Mr Willes was the doyen of racing writers of the time. He was no respecter of persons and he and Rous were no strangers to controversy or to each other. In commenting on the result of the Admiral's handicap for the Cesarewitch the previous year Mr Willes had written: 'His friend's horse won, the one of which he was part owner ran second, and the horse left him as a legacy and which he sold got third.'

Those were words the Admiral was unlikely to forget; nor did he. 'From the moment Mr Willes penned those sentences he was a marked man,' a contemporary wrote, and he was right. Mr Willes's article commenting on the Tarragona enquiry and the events leading up to it is too long to quote here, but it was vitriolic to an extreme. 'Are we in England or Venetia?' he enquired at one point, and went on to state that the names of surgeons skilled in the treatment of gunshot wounds were being eagerly sought at Newmarket. These, however, were only minor gems in a polemic that went into every one of the Admiral's errors and castigated them in detail.

When the Jockey Club next met Lord Winchilsea (who had also had occasion to suffer under Mr Willes's lash) drew the members' attention to the article. Lord Stradbroke and Charles Greville argued that it was not expedient for the Club to take notice of what appeared in the public prints. They were over-ruled, and a second motion, proposed by Lord Winchilsea and seconded by Admiral Rous that Mr Willes be required to make an apology for certain offensive expressions used by him, was carried. By a strange coincidence at the same meeting Lord Stamford brought forward a motion to have M'George removed from his position as starter, but on being informed that his son would officiate at the spring meetings of the following year he withdrew it.

The request for an apology was immediately conveyed to Mr Willes, who promptly refused to give it. Whereupon he became the recipient of the following letter:

Newmarket. Nov 3. 1862.
Sir, — I beg to acquaint you that, at the adjourned meeting of the Jockey Club, held here on the 31st ult., after your letter to me of that date had been read, it was resolved:—

'That Mr Willes, having been required to make an apology for certain offensive expressions used by him in a letter signed "Argus" published in *The Morning Post* and not having done so, be warned off the lands and property of the Jockey Club at Newmarket.'

Following this Rous took the extraordinary step of sending to *The Morning Post* much of the correspondence he had had with the various interested parties. In his covering letter he attempted to justify his conduct throughout the affair and to link the Reindeer matter with the Tarragona case. He ended this letter with the statement: 'I have thought it my duty in the difficult and responsible position I fill as Steward of the Jockey Club to make these facts known to the public.'

This hasty action only made matters worse for him. All the parties named in the correspondence and many others who felt themselves in some way concerned in it leapt into the fray, publishing letters denying his accusations and in some cases calling for apologies in no uncertain terms. Rous's conduct of the whole affair was made to appear even worse by the facts disclosed in the correspondence that one of those whose evidence he had relied upon to bear him out in the Reindeer matter had withdrawn his previous statements on the grounds that they were given under duress by Rous, and that Rous, in view of this, had issued a sort of guarded apology to Burnaby.

Letters now began to fly thick and fast. Lord Garlies took up his brother's cause and in thunderous terms demanded an apology from Rous. Stewart himself published a letter referring to Rous's 'extraordinary perversion of the facts'. 'Admiral Rous is, or rather, was, an old friend of mine', another letter began, while a third commenced: 'I am greatly astonished at Admiral Rous re-opening the Reindeer affair after he had fully apologised, through me, to Colonel Burnaby for his mistaken verdict of the bets. . . .' It was left, however, to *The Morning Post*, still smarting under the treatment meted out to its chief racing correspondent, to apply the final strokes of the lash to Rous's back. The *Post* devoted a leader to the case — and to Rous:

It now appears that he has been humoured so far that he has been induced to believe in his own infallibility. He arbitrarily acts down a number of gentlemen as swindlers of the worst type; and, having pledged himself to that opinion, he sets to work to prove himself right by methods which can find no excuse in any right thinking mind. . . . It is impossible to peruse the letters which we publish in another column, without feeling the warmest sympathy for the various gentlemen who have been the victims of the reckless prejudice and unjustifiable attacks of this painfully mistaken and intensely mischievous meddler.

The reflections on the character of two of his officers as made by Rous were so grave, and the verdict of the committee so unsatisfactory, that the Commander in Chief, the Duke of Cambridge, set up a military court of enquiry to investigate the charges that Captain Annesley and Colonel Burnaby 'had made a sham match and flash bets thereon at Newmarket'. The court returned a finding completely clearing both officers.

CHAPTER 5

Chetwynd v. Durham:
A Scandal of the Eighties

I AM CERTAIN that it is as much a mater of regret to the members of the Jockey Club as it is to me that some men, equal to us in social position and racing influence, have failed to maintain the fair reputation of the turf.... Do not let us strain at a gnat and swallow a camel; that is the acme of imbecility. The higher a man's position on the turf the more needful it is that he should be above reproach. If we find that such a man or such men continue with impunity to break the rules of racing law and the code of honour among gentlemen, let us treat them as they deserve to be treated — as unfit to mix with us and associate with us in the sport we love....

These words were spoken by the Earl of Durham when making the customary speech at the Gimcrack dinner of 1887. They created a sensation, as indeed they were intended to.

Lord Durham was a young man of thirty-two. He had only been active in racing for six years, his career as an owner having started in 1881. He was not then a steward of the Jockey Club and had only recently been elected a member. Then as always, he was intensely ambitious, domineering, forthright, and indifferent to the opinions of others. Later he was to become the fourth of the great dictators of the Turf,

89

serving no fewer than five terms as a steward. He was as ruthless in pursuit of what he felt to be right as any of his predecessors, and just as unheeding of advice or moderate counsels. This speech was his first flamboyant step on the course which was to carry him forward to his long reign of despotism in the corridors of racing power.

Everyone connected with racing realised immediately at whom the thinly veiled allusions were aimed. Sir George Chetwynd had been senior steward of the Jockey Club in 1878. He was a man of long lineage and distinguished bearing, and his family had been active on the Turf since 1709. He owned, ran and managed a large string of horses and was probably the most knowledgeable of all the senior racing men of the day. Because of his skill and experience he did not suffer fools gladly and those who attempted to presume upon his acquaintance to pick his brains or to parade their little learning before him suffered under the cutting lash of his tongue. His private fortune was insignificant in the context of the time and quite inadequate to support his way of life. In order to augment it and to keep himself afloat he gambled, heavily and successfully.

For some time before Lord Durham made the Gimcrack speech rumours had been prevalent that the in-and-out running of certain of Sir George's horses owed nothing to chance and everything to calculation. George Lambton, whose testimony in this instance, since he was the younger brother and ardent champion of Lord Durham, must be treated with some caution, tells how on one occasion in the Jockey Club rooms at Newmarket Chetwynd remarked to the owner of a winning outsider: 'Thank God, horses in my stable don't start at 100—6 and break all the backers,' only to receive the reply: 'No, George, but your horses often start at 100—6 and *don't* win.'

Chetwynd's horses were trained by Richard Sherrard and his stable jockey was Charles Wood. Wood was brilliant and had ranked second only to Archer in his prime. He was very fond of money and, unfortunately for him, not too scrupulous as to how he acquired it. Unusually for a jockey, when he had acquired it he employed it skilfully and well. At the time Lord Durham made his speech Wood was in affluent circumstances. He was the largest shareholder — with 6,000 shares — in a prosperous cooperage company; he owned two public houses in the Newmarket area and had £10,000 invested in the funds. These holdings alone amounted to a considerable fortune for one whose riding fees amounted on average to approximately £2,000 a year. But he also owned a small thirty-acre stud farm and had bought for £10,000 Sir John Astley's Newmarket property, which he had converted into an up-to-date, palatial training establishment named Chetwynd House in honour of his chief patron, and which he leased to Sherrard. It was there that Sherrard trained for Sir George and many other leading and aristocratic owners. Wood, however, was always greedy for more and his reputation on the Turf was bad. He was accused behind his back of almost every crime a jockey can commit — stopping horses, running a 'jockeys' ring' to deceive owners and trainers, running horses in-and-out, rowing in with bookmakers for his own profit, and many more. Unquestionably at least some of the accusations were true. He also owned a number of horses himself whose running played ducks and drakes with the form book, and it was largely because of him that in 1887 the Jockey Club introduced a rule that no licensed jockey could own or have an interest in a racehorse. In 1888, after Lord Durham's speech but before the hearing of the action arising from it, his licence to ride was withdrawn.

Lord Durham's success on the Turf up to the time he made his speech had been singularly undistinguished — in fact that victory in the Gimcrack had been his only worthwhile win. Also, at the outset of his career at least, he lent himself avidly to the antagonism in racing between north and south, the extremes of which were even then beginning to die out.

It has been generally accepted that his motives in making the speech were purely altruistic and that he was driven solely by a desire to cleanse what he saw as the Augean stables of racing. If so, he chose a strange way of doing it, and a conflict of personality may well have played a part in what he said and did, for there was at least a suspicion of personal antagonism between himself and Sir George. This may have been fostered by the narrow and unexpected defeat of his horse Sylvan at New-

91

market by Sir George's Plantagenet, ridden by Wood. Durham had £1,000 on Sylvan and, according to Sir George, he came up to him in the luncheon-room afterwards and said: 'You have broken me.'

In addition, on his own admission he had crossed verbal swords with Sir George about the running of Sir George's Fullerton, the horse at the centre of his accusations of pulling and stopping and in-and-out running. 'I told Sir George', he said, 'that I thought he ought to enquire of his jockey how he had ridden his horse, as I thought the riding of Wood was inconsistent.' He did not give Sir George's response to these impertinences from a young and inexperienced racing man, but it can be readily imagined and can have done little to improve relations between the two men.

Durham had also had words with Lord Lurgan, a friend of Chetwynd's who trained with Sherrard. Durham had run a horse of his, Vagabond, on successive days at Doncaster. On the first day he was down the field but on the second he came out and won the Cleveland Stakes at 10—1. Lurgan laughingly said to him that he ought to be had up before the stewards, at which Durham turned on him and said: 'You, coming from Sherrard's stable, are the last man in the world to say such a thing.' Taken aback, Lurgan said he was only chaffing. Durham's comment was that that was the sort of chaff he did not like.

Durham received far from universal approval from members of the Jockey Club of the action he had taken in making his accusations public. Many could not understand his deliberate courting of publicity and thought the whole thing savoured of washing dirty linen in public. 'It was a bold attack but it went too far and left his flanks unguarded,' was the comment of one well-known and well-connected Gentleman Rider who was present, and many others felt that the matter, if ventilated at all, should have been done through the counsels of the Jockey Club itself.

Once his attention had been drawn to the content of the speech, Sir George had no doubt that it referred to him, for Durham had gone much further than the remarks quoted above. He had continued, in elaboration:

There is a well-known and what the sporting press calls a fashionable and aristocratic racing stable that has been conspicuous throughout the season for the constant and inexplicable in-and-out running of its horses. Their running has surprised and disgusted the public. . . . But the darkest part of the matter is this — that the owners, or nominal owners, of the horses to which I am alluding win large stakes when their horses are successful and do not lose much when they are beaten. . . .

Sir George's first instinct was to challenge Durham to a duel, but he was soon persuaded that this was an outmoded method of preserving his honour. Instead, he sent his brother along to Lord Durham to ask him to make clear once and for all whether the statements referred to him. Durham's response was immediate and unequivocal — yes, he said, his remarks had been aimed at Sir George, they were true and accurate and he would not withdraw a word. His actual words were: 'I do mean to accuse Sir George Chetwynd of being connected with a series of malpractices which are contrary to the rules of racing.' He then wrote to the Jockey Club:

Gentlemen,
With a view to relieving Sir George Chetwynd and the Stewards and members of the Club of legal difficulties. . . .
I now offer to hand to the stewards a copy of my speech at York so that he [Sir George] may have no excuse in not at once bringing an action at law against me in which the truth of my statement may be fully investigated. . . .

The matter had now received such publicity that it obviously could not be left to a private investigation by the Jockey Club. There was only one course open to Sir George — he issued a writ for slander and libel, claiming £20,000 damages. From that moment luck, which had served him so well in the past, began to run against him.

Just before Durham's Gimcrack speech Wood had taken

a libel action against *The Licensed Victualler's Gazette* which had flatly accused him of pulling certain horses. The trial had been reduced almost to a farce by the judge's open ignorance of racing, his ill-considered comments and his flagrant prejudice against the plaintiff. As a result, although the jury returned a verdict in favour, Wood only received a farthing damages.

Naturally enough the judge's conduct came in for considerable criticism from the racing world. Consequently Lord Durham's advisers approached Sir George's with a view to removing his action from the courts and submitting it to arbitration. Sir George's solicitor and counsel advised him to agree and he did so. He was afterwards told that the Lord Chief Justice 'shook his head' when he heard of the decision. If so, he was right, for it was a most unwise course to take. The arbitrators, however knowledgeable they might be about racing, would have no appreciation of the legal issues involved. Although the matter might look straightforward at first sight there were difficult legal questions involved, especially as to the admissibility of certain evidence upon which the arbitrators were not competent to decide. Nor did they have the assistance of a legal assessor sitting with them to advise them on points of law. Furthermore there would be no summing up and no appeal.

The final choice of arbitrators comprised the three stewards of the Jockey Club, the Earl of March, Mr James Lowther and Prince Soltikoff. Lowther was in the chair. Although Lowther had been called to the bar he had never practised, but had turned his talents to a parliamentary career. He had held high office, including Chief Secretary to the Lord Lieutenant of Ireland. Here at a difficult time he had not proved a success. After being defeated in the 1880 election, although re-elected some fifteen months later, he appeared to lose interest in Parliamentary affairs and he devoted more and more of his time to the counsels of the Jockey Club to which he had been elected in 1877, serving his first term as a steward in 1880. At the time of the hearing he had been breeding and owning racehorses for sixteen years, though without great success, and was serving his second term as senior steward. He was a man of the utmost rectitude who demanded of others the same high standard of personal conduct which he set himself.

The Earl of March, although a steward of the Jockey Club, was more distinguished as a politician than as a racing man. He had delivered a qualified rebuke to Sir George over the running of one of his horses and a moderately heated correspondence had ensued, so the propriety of his sitting at all was questionable.

Prince Soltikoff had had a colourful career. Born and brought up in St Petersburg, he had worked in the Russian Foreign Office before enlisting as a private in the Crimean War. Commissioned from the ranks, he had been in the forefront of every battle in the campaign. When peace was declared he came to England and fell in love with the country, and especially with English racing. He built himself a house near Newmarket called Kremlin Lodge where he settled down to devote all his time to horses and racing. In 1867 he was elected a member of the Jockey Club and was a steward at the time of the hearing. Not noticeably successful on the Turf, he was nevertheless universally liked and respected, but with his background he could hardly be expected to appreciate the niceties of English law or evidence likely to be presented at the hearing of this difficult case.

To make matters worse for Sir George, his adversary had secured by far the more powerful team of lawyers. His instructing solicitor was Sir George Lewis, probably the most famous legal adviser ever to the nobility and whose name is associated with virtually every society scandal during his long career. It is quite possible that Lord Durham had consulted Lewis before he made the speech, and that the speech itself, together with the letter to the Jockey Club, had been edited by Lewis and his advisers. Certainly the letter gives every evidence of having been drafted by a legal hand.

Lewis employed as his leading counsel Sir Charles Russell, one of the forensic giants of all time. Sir Charles was an Ulster Roman Catholic who had fought his way to pre-eminence at the English bar by tenacity, application and an unrivalled talent for pure advocacy, especially in cross-examination. He was a powerful, ruthless advocate who could browbeat juries into giving him the verdict he wanted by the sheer exercise of his overbearing personality. He was also prone to pushing the ethics of his profession to their very limits and some, especially his many enemies, said well beyond them. If ever there was a man uniquely equipped to dominate a board of arbitrators unversed in the law it was he. He was assisted by Charles Matthews QC, whose effeminate appearance concealed deadly gifts as a cross-examiner.

Against this formidable array Sir George was advised by his personal solicitor, a Mr Sydney, who had nothing like Lewis's experience. Sydney briefed as his leader Sir Henry James, an excellent lawyer and an ingenious pleader but whose methods were those of subtlety and persuasion, utterly unlike those of Russell. He was at another grave disadvantage in this case — he knew nothing of racing. Russell, on the other hand, was a racing man, and had mastered all the technicalities of the sport. James's junior was Rufus Isaacs, then at the beginning of a career in which he would be Lord Chief Justice and Viceroy of India. His rôle in this case was confined to an intense study of *Ruff's* and other guides to the Turf so that he could make his leader conversant with the reading of form, the intricacies of handicapping and the jargon of the racing world.

It is a measure of the importance which the two leaders attached to this case that, although both were actively engaged at the time on opposite sides of the Parnell Commission, throughout the twelve days of the case's hearing they devoted the whole of their energies to it.

Whether or not Sir George's morals on the racecourse or alleged lack of them committed him to malpractice — and malice and rumour will always point a finger at success — his openness in revealing every facet of his dealings with Wood and Sherrard, both to the defence during the pleadings and interrogatories and to the arbitrators during the case, displayed a nicety of honour and a degree of candour far beyond the bounds of prudence. This was especially true when he was opposed by an advocate of Russell's ruthlessness who was ready and willing to take advantage of any opening which could be used to discredit an adversary.

Sir George even went to the extent of retrieving from Wood and Sherrard all the letters he had written them over the years preceding the allegations, and putting them into evidence. He had no obligation to do this, but he even insisted on disclosing a letter to Wood marked 'Private' which may well have done him irremediable damage. Whether his legal advisers protested and he over-ruled them we shall never know. It should not and need not have been done.

Having decided on a policy of full disclosure, Chetwynd placed all his betting-books, bank accounts and other records into his opponents' hands. He also stood firmly by Wood and Sherrard, stating that he held to his belief in the ability and integrity of them both. In this, too, his loyalty and standards of personal honour in his dealings with servants must have outrun his wisdom, for he had been in court throughout the case of Wood v. The Licensed Victualler's Gazette and must have learnt something of Wood's deviousness, even if, as alleged, he did not know it already.

The delivery of the pleadings and interrogatories had taken a long time and it was not until June 1889 that the three arbitrators sat. The case attracted enormous interest, especially in society and among racing men. Sides were being openly taken and most of the seniors, including the Prince of Wales, who had no reason to love either the law or lawyers, supported Sir George. The younger set, on the other hand, some of whom had suffered from Sir George's cutting comments, came out in favour of Durham.

As the time approached for the hearing to begin the court-room and its approaches were crowned with society figures jostling for seats. The accommodation in No. 5 Queen's Bench Court was quite inadequate and many were left outside when Sir Henry James rose to open the case for the plaintiff. In his speech he dealt in detail with the charges of 'in-and-out running', especially those concerning Fullerton where the main weight of this attack lay. As to the allegations of aiding and abetting malpractices, he made the point and made it well that

97

here the defence had cast its net so wide that it included cognisance of malpractice with horses other than his own. Since this was so then the charges, Sir Henry said, applied equally to the owners of those other horses, some of whom bore names distinguished on the Turf — Sir George Arthur, Lord Lurgan, General Owen Williams among them. Did his learned friend, Sir Henry enquired, now intend to withdraw these implied charges against these men?

'I will as regards General Owen Williams,' Russell growled.

In effect Durham was charging these owners with complicity, but had chosen for reasons of his own to make an example of Sir George and, that being so, Sir Henry enquired, why had these others not been brought before the stewards of the Jockey Club? Sir Henry was, however, perhaps not so astute in nailing his or rather Sir George's colours to the mast in what he described as the 'minor matters' of his client's involvement with Sherrard and Wood. Sir George, he said, still believed Sherrard to be an honest man. 'The position of Sir George towards Sherrard is this — he gives him his fullest confidence, consults him as to his horses and there was in the past some approach to a general agency in dealing with his horses in his absence.' As to Wood, Sir George, he said, never had the slightest ground for believing that Wood had any interest in the horses in Sherrard's stable. He had never heard of any such interest until these charges were made and, after making enquiries, he was assured that no such interest existed. 'According to my brief not a hair or a tail of these horses belonged to Wood.'

When he had concluded, the arbitrators adjourned for lunch and then Sir George went into the box. Tall, handsome, perfectly turned out and entirely self-composed, he made an impressive figure and he gave his direct evidence in answer to his counsel's questions clearly and well. When Russell rose to examine a hush fell on the crowded court-room. It was generally anticipated that this was to be a clash of titans, as indeed it turned out to be. Sir George was a well-born, highly intelligent man, utterly unlike the usual run of ignorant and uneducated witnesses of the day whom Russell could browbeat into sub-mission and whose testimony he could tear to shreds. Sir George was, moreover, a master of the subject on which he was to be cross-examined — racing and the performance of racehorses. In every respect, therefore, he could be classed as an expert witness and as many counsel know to their cost the testimony of expert witnesses is notoriously difficult to shake.

Russell's attack fell mainly under three heads — firstly that Sir George had broken the rules by betting for Wood and aiding and abetting him in his wagers; secondly that he was a party to Wood's ownership of horses again in contravention of the rules of racing; thirdly and most importantly, that he was a party to and cognisant of Wood's stopping his horses in order to obtain lenient handicapping and long prices when they ran to win. The meat of this last accusation lay in the performances of Sir George's good horse, Fullerton.

It was, however, typical of Russell that almost his first question was an unfair effort to discredit Sir George at the outset. 'Have you filled the office of steward of the Jockey Club?' Russell asked him.

'Yes, in about 1878, I think.'

'One who has served the office of steward is eligible for election at a later period?'

'Yes.'

'Have you served more than once?'

'No.'

This question was clearly aimed at creating the impression that since he had not been re-elected Sir George was in some way suspect by his peers. Later in the case Lowther referred to this question which indeed he should have done when it was made, by saying: 'I was nearly calling attention to the remark at the time, and thought that some impression might be created that some reflection might be cast on a member not being re-elected.' Since this was, of course, exactly the impression Russell wished to create one may pause to wonder why Lowther waited so long. It was again typical of Russell that he immediately attempted to explain his question away in a manner best suited to soothe the arbitrator and benefit his client's case. 'Not at all,' he said. 'I wished to see what was the extent of Sir George's experience and fix his position and responsibility in relation to public racing.' If this was really his intention, he was soon to receive a demonstration of both these things in Sir George's answers to his questions.

As to the matter of his permitting Wood to bet, and indeed betting for him in certain cases, Sir George was on firm ground and was able to prove it. There had been two notices in the *Racing Calendar* about betting, one in December 1883 and the other in December 1887, just before Lord Durham's Gimcrack speech. The 1883 notice merely referred to jockeys 'betting largely' and Sir George was able to show from his betting-books that he had never had more than £50 on for Wood and had told both the Earl of March and Mr Lowther in their capacity as stewards that he was betting in this and other similar and smaller sums for Wood. No objection to his doing so had been made. The 1887 notice had been published in the last *Calendar* before the Gimcrack speech — a coincidence which suggests that Durham may have had a hand in its drafting to suit his own purposes. This second notice prohibited jockeys betting at all and Sir George had observed the prohibition, as he was again able to prove. It was once more typical of Russell's style of advocacy that he attempted to confuse the witness and the arbitrators by treating the two notices as one and, without explicitly saying so, to suggest that the earlier notice prohibited jockeys from betting at all.

'Supposing', Russell said, 'that you put on — I am not suggesting that you did — some money for your jockey and he put on money through other channels which you did not know anything about ... it might be worth his while to square other jockeys?'

'Yes, in that case; but this is an insinuation you are putting to me, because I do not know of anything of the kind.'

'I am not suggesting for a moment that you do.' (But he was later to suggest that very thing.) 'I am calling attention to the rule against betting.'

'I never understood the notice to mean that jockeys were not to bet at all. ... I thought that the notice meant that jockeys were not to bet high — for instance as much as £300 or £400 on a race.'

100

'Do you think that since the events that have transpired in 1887 racing has been straighter?'

'No, I do not.'

'Do you think that there has been more or less inexplicable in-and-out running?'

'Inexplicable is a funny word, because a man may have an explanation which is a very bad one.'

'And your impression is that a strict enforcement of the new rule against jockeys betting would have a bad effect?'

'I do not know of any new rule.'

'I call it a new rule. '

'It is not a new rule. It is a notice put in the *Calendar* and it has never been made a rule of racing.'

'As an ex-steward and a member of the Jockey Club you would not consider it right to be a party to a course of practice contrary to the notice?' Russell was clearly trying to suggest that both notices prohibited jockeys betting at all, but Sir George would have none of it.

'I thought it was not contrary to the notice,' he said. 'The notice was about jockeys betting largely.'

But Russell persisted in his attempt to discredit him on the 1887 notice. 'You no doubt think it would be objectionable and condemnable to be a party to a course of conduct contrary to that rule?' he asked, but he failed to specify which rule.

'That certainly cannot apply to any course of conduct I pursued,' was the firm reply.

Here Russell became nettled, a frequent occurrence when he was not getting the answers he required from his witness. 'I wish you would be good enough to attend to the question put to you for a moment,' he said testily. 'Irrespective of yourself, you would consider it condemnable to countervail the notice?'

At this point Lowther was driven to intervene and set the record straight. 'You, Sir Charles Russell,' he said, 'will bear in mind that in the original notice the words "betting largely" were used. One notice in other words prohibited large betting, and the other notice prohibited betting of any kind.'

Russell then abandoned that line of cross-examination,

leaving Sir George the victor, but when he turned to the question of jockeys owning racehorses he was on much stronger ground, for Sir George was very vulnerable here and both of them must have known it.

In December 1883 the Jockey Club had published a notice to the effect that licenses to ride would only be granted to jockeys who were 'not owners or part owners of any racehorses'. The notice was qualified by the statement that leave would be given to one or two jockeys to own one or more horses. Wood owned several valuable horses. He applied for leave to keep them and this, together with his licence to ride, was refused until such a time as he had rid himself of the horses. Both Wood and Sir George felt aggrieved by this since other jockeys received permission to retain their horses. Since Sir George's represent-ations to the stewards proved unavailing and as Sherrard, Wood and himself all wished to keep the horses in the stable, Wood offered the horses to Sir George at Sherrard's valuation. There were six horses and Sherrard put £2,300 on the lot. Sir George did not have £2,300 just then, nor anything like it, and apparently he had no means of raising it. He there-fore wrote the following letter to Wood — the damning letter marked 'Private' which was put into evidence and read in court.

Dear Sir,
I am quite sensible of your wish that I should lose nothing by the horses, and that if I take them I propose accepting the terms you suggest in your letter in a friendly way — viz., that if they turn out badly we shall not stick to the price agreed on now £2,300 but arrange between us and Sherrard what will be fair for both parties. *The arrangement in a friendly way has nothing to do with anyone else and no one need know it.* [Author's italics.] You sell me the horses for £2,300 with their engagements, and they become my property now. It is nothing to anyone else if you come to me and say, 'I am sorry so-and-so has not turned out well, I will give you so much back.' I enclose a letter for you to forward to Messrs Weatherby; that will end the matter.

The letter to Weatherby's was short and to the point and almost equally damning. It ran as follows:

Gentlemen,
I have disposed of all my horses to Sir George Chetwynd.
Mr Sherrard has bought my half so will you please send me
a licence to ride.

To make matters worse for Sir George, although he did take possession of the horses immediately and from that moment paid all their entry fees, forfeits, training fees and expenses, he did not pay Wood the purchase price for nearly two years and when he did it was reduced to £1,200 as some had turned out badly.

Here indeed was material for Russell's cross-examination and he made the most of it. First he read out a letter from Wood offering Sir George the horses at £2,300 in which he said: 'So far as the money is concerned, why, pay for them when they win for you. If they do not turn out well, I shall of course, take nothing for them. . . .' 'I ask you,' Russell said in his most menacing tones, 'as master of the stable, and still more in your position as a member of the Jockey Club and as an ex-steward of that Club, do you think that was a proper arrangement to enter into with a jockey?'

'There was no arrangement at all,' Sir George answered. 'I bought the horses.' He may have done, but on the face of it it was a very curious transaction as Russell was promptly at pains to point out by reading in full the letter marked 'Private' and the enclosure for forwarding to Weatherby's. 'I must ask your deliberate opinion,' he said. 'Do you think that if that letter which I have read was forwarded to Messrs Weatherby for inspection by the stewards, together with the letter which you forwarded, that it would be regarded as a compliance with the rule, and a sale outright to you?'

'Most distinctly I think it would. It was a sale outright to me.' It was a brave answer but not a very convincing one.

Russell pursued it. 'Was, or was not, the result of this transaction to give Wood an interest in those horses?' he asked.

'No, I swear it was not.'

'Was it not obvious that it was?'

'I ought to have framed the letter better because you have twisted it and turned it.'

'I assure you I have not.'

'I will not say that, but you put another construction on what I meant when I wrote it. I give you my word of honour that I bought those horses outright from Wood, that I owned every hair of their tails, and from the time I bought those horses Wood had nothing whatever to do with them.'

'Let me ask you, why should the horses not have been put up to auction, and if you were able to buy them and pay for them, buy them at their market price?'

'The thing was hurried,' Sir George answered, and then gave the reasons which undoubtedly lay behind the whole strange transaction: 'Wood had to get rid of his horses to get his licence; I was anxious to help them; Sherrard and Wood wanted the horses in the stable; Wood wanted to ride them, and Sherrard did not want to part with them. When Wood got rid of his horses he would get his licence.'

That concluded the cross-examination concerning the transfer of the horses from Wood to Sir George, and it left Russell a clear victor — whichever way you looked at it the transaction was a dubious one. Sir Henry James was quick to point out that by taking over the horses and paying all their expenses legally the property had passed to Sir George and he was therefore their absolute owner, but the arbitrators were unlikely to pay much attention to the finer points of the law of contract.

Then came the crux of the whole case — the running of Fullerton. Here the battle really joined since the meat of the case or, to put it technically, the sting of the libel was the accusation that Sir George had connived at the pulling of Fullerton in certain races in order to make money by betting.

The running of Fullerton was vitally important since Russell opened his cross-examination on this aspect of the matter by saying flatly: 'I want to go through this running and you, sir, will be relieved when I say this is the only horse whose running I intend to trouble you with in detail.'

104

It was a fact that the sporting press had in the latter part of 1887 made marked comments on the running of Fullerton and on 6 December, immediately before the Gimcrack speech — again the coincidence of dates is curious — Weatherby's had written to Sir George on behalf of the stewards of the Jockey Club, asking for an explanation. Sir George's reply had been uncompromising: 'I shall be obliged to you,' he wrote, 'if you will request them [the stewards] to hold a meeting as soon as possible, and that they will send me word to attend, that I may prove to them in the most conclusive manner what foul calumnies the said comments are.'

'Was that statement true that invidious comments had been repeatedly and publicly made?' Russell asked him.

'No,' was the answer. 'I only heard one.'

'Do you mean *viva voce*?'

'No, I never heard one *viva voce*. I should like to have heard a man say it to me.' When he said this, Sir George turned round in the witness box and stared directly at a man sitting in the well of the court who had been named to him as one of his traducers. The man hurriedly left his seat and walked out of court, not to return.

These first questions and answers set the tone for the whole of the cross-examination concerning the running of Fullerton. Here indeed was a conflict of experts — the greatest advocate of the day pitted against the most knowledgeable racing man of his time. The clash was what everyone was waiting for and the outcome did not disappoint them. The cross-examination was immensely long and detailed. Every item in it is fascinating to anyone interested in the cut and thrust of legal battle or the study of racing lore. Only fractions can be given here; enough however can be set down to show that Russell more than met his match and that he did not perhaps know quite as much about racing as he thought he did.

Fullerton had been beaten in the Lincoln Handicap by a colt called Oberon. They met again in the Babraham Plate at the Newmarket Craven meeting, where Fullerton reversed the placings. There was a difference of 7 lb in Fullerton's favour in the second race. In answer to Russell's question about the difference in the weights compared with the Lincoln, Sir George said that he thought that 7lb would have brought them together.

'You must not ask me to accept that,' Russell said. 'What makes you say it?'

'Wood told me the horse was going so fast at the finish.'

'Upon the running, as one reads it, and apart from the information which your jockey gave you as to his impressions of the race, 7lb would not bring Fullerton and Oberon together?' Russell said.

'No, not to anyone who did not know what I did,' was the candid and correct reply.

Russell then read an account of the race from *The Sportsman*, which appeared to suggest that Fullerton had been pulled in the Lincoln in order to get the resulting advantage at the weights.

'You backed him to win £350?' Russell asked.

'Yes, and according to this race he could not have won the Lincoln Handicap.'

'Let me refer you to a paper you have said you do read — *The Sportsman*.'

'I prefer to give my own opinion against *The Sportsman*.' Sir George paused for a moment and then made a succinct comment which was not lost on the racing men in court: 'Oberon is a thief.'

Russell, however, was not prepared to leave it there. 'Was it not a severe finish between the two and did not Fullerton win by staying better?' he said, clearly trying to imply that Fullerton should have won the Lincoln.

'I think Oberon should have won the Babraham,' replied Sir George, and he backed up his statement by revealing that he had had a saver of £110 — £80 on Oberon.

Russell had not done very well so far in questioning the running of Fullerton but he now proceeded to do a great deal worse. 'The next race in which the horse [Fullerton] ran was the Jubilee Stakes at Kempton,' Russell said. 'You backed Fullerton here, did you not?'

Sir George agreed that he had put on £200, and that the length of the Jubilee Stakes was one mile.

'Is it important to get your horse well off to be well placed at the bend?' Russell asked.

'No,' was the firm reply. 'It is not important.'

'Why?' Russell asked, which, in view of the answer to which he left himself open, and which he received, was a dreadful mistake.

'Archer and Fordham both told me in discussing this course', Sir George said, 'that if a man makes the running to get round the bend first, something always catches them, and they preferred to wait and take their chance of getting through. That opinion was the result of races they had ridden in.' Archer and Fordham were the two cracks of the day, and Sir George could hardly have quoted weightier authority.

'Did you not give Wood orders to get well off in front and to have a good place at the turn?'

'I suggested those orders to him.'

Once more Russell was becoming exasperated. 'A master does not suggest orders; a master gives his servant orders,' he snapped. It was a comment, not a question, and Sir George, given the opportunity to elaborate his answer, took full advantage of it.

'I went to Wood,' he continued, 'and said, "I know nothing about Fullerton; but he apparently ran very gamely against Oberon in the Babraham Plate, and therefore I think, considering the quantity of weight Bendigo has got to give Fullerton, it would be well to get off and lie in a good place"; but Wood's answer was, "I would much rather wait as I think speed is his best point"; and I said, "You ought to know more than I do; ride him as you like."'

'Did you not tell your friends that you had given Wood orders to jump off, and to take a good place at the bend?'

'No, I did not.'

'As a matter of fact, had Wood a good place at the bend?'

'No, he had not.'

'What do you think now of your suggested orders against Wood's tactics?'

'I think mine would have been the best.'

'Fullerton was fourth, I believe?'

'Yes, he came up with a wet sail.'

'Just beaten for third place?'

107

All this, of course, was to suggest that Sir George and Wood had stopped Fullerton, but again, from his knowledge of how the race had been run, Sir George had a ready explanation. 'Yes,' he said. 'Watts told me that there were two horses in front of Fullerton and Bendigo and they crossed in front of Fullerton and Bendigo got inside.'

Having failed to make much progress here, Russell went on to Fullerton's next two races, the Manchester Cup and the Wilton Plate. Fullerton had finished in front of King Monmouth in the first and been beaten by him in the second. 'You said yesterday', Russell said, 'that Fullerton's best distance was a mile.'

'My opinion is so.'

'You also told us that the heavy ground at Lincoln jeopardized Fullerton's chance. Was not the ground very heavy going at Manchester upon the Cup day?'

'No. It was perfect going. It did not rain until the night after the Manchester Cup.'

Again Russell tried to retrieve his mistake: 'Is it not nearly always heavy going at Manchester?' he asked.

And once more Sir George had his trump card ready. 'No,' he said. 'Not in the summer and this was the summer meeting.'

'A mile is King Monmouth's best distance, is it not?' Russell continued, turning to the Wilton Plate after having had the worst of the exchange concerning the Manchester Cup.

'No, I should think not,' Sir George replied. 'I should say a mile and a half is his best distance. I have seen him win a big race over a mile and three quarters.'

'Was the going heavy in the Wilton Plate?'

'Yes, dreadfully heavy.'

'The heavy ground did not prevent your backing Fullerton?'

'No, but it ought to have done.'

'Do you suggest that Fullerton objects to heavy ground more than any other horse ordinarily does?'

'Most certainly I suggest it; I am positive of it.'

And so it went on. When Russell sat down he had subjected Sir George to one of the most gruelling cross-examinations he had ever delivered in his long career, but he had failed to shake him. Russell had to a certain degree the volatility of his race and at the conference that night he was profoundly depressed. It is said that he suggested an approach should be made for a settlement. Certainly rumours were rife that a compromise was being negotiated and one paper actually announced it, without mentioning the terms. Durham, however, whatever his faults, had both pugnacity and courage, and he would never admit to have been in the wrong, especially in public. Backed by Sir George Lewis, he insisted on the case being fought out. When Sherrard and Wood were called as witnesses things began to look very different.

Neither the trainer nor the jockey had the mental equipment or education to stand up to stringent cross-examinations from such skilled practitioners as Russell and Matthews. More important still, it soon emerged that they had between them been up to some singularly shady deals which they very clumsily attempted to conceal. These attempts only made matters worse for them and counsel in cross-examination stripped them bare and showed them up for what they were.

Although Sherrard had a hundred horses in training and had enjoyed considerable success with them it soon became apparent that he was a mere figurehead behind whom Wood controlled the operations of the stable. It also emerged that many of the transactions concerning the purchase and sale of horses were purely paper ones — if even that — and that a considerable number of the horses running in certain owners' names were in fact Wood's property. Where the attack failed, however, was in its attempts to tie in their activities and malpractices with Sir George Chetwynd and to prove his knowledge of and participation in them. In the case of Wood something far worse than mere ownership of horses was revealed — he was forced to admit that he had taken money from winning owners, having ridden horses belonging to others in the same race. This was a clear indication that he had been paid to stop his own mounts. The most glaring instance of this was the Cambridgeshire of 1884, won by Mr Hammond's Florence trained by Sherrard. Wood was engaged by John Porter to ride the Duke of Westminster's Sandiway. Porter fancied Sandiway, who had finished second in the St Leger, a race Porter thought she might well have won if she had not suffered interference in the running. In the Cambridgeshire, however, she ran unplaced to Florence. After the race it was widely alleged that Wood had accepted a present of £500 from Mr Hammond for stopping Sandiway. Here is how Russell destroyed Wood on this subject and shattered whatever pretence the remainder of his evidence might have had to reliability, and how, also, he attempted to drag Sir George's name into the transaction:

'After the race did Mr Hammond give you £500?' Russell asked Wood.

Instead of the flat denial that might have been expected if he had not committed the offence, Wood temporised. 'I cannot say,' he answered.

Russell must have realized immediately that he had his witness cornered. 'If Sir George Chetwynd asked you whether any present was made you would have told him the truth?' he said.

'I should say very likely I did,' was the evasive answer given once again.

'If he said anything, did you tell him that you got the £500 or not?'

'I might have said it and I might not.'

'Did you tell him the truth?'

'I think so.'

'Did you tell him that you got £500?'

'I am not sure; it is such a long time ago.'

'And the truth is that you did get the £500?'

'Very likely.'

'When Sir George Chetwynd spoke to you about this matter did he ask to see your bank book?'

'No. Excuse me but I am not certain that Mr Hammond did give me this £500.' Wood was trying to wriggle out of his former admissions or near admissions, but he was not having much success and Russell was determined to pin him to the wall.

'Will you swear that you did not receive a present of £500 from Mr Hammond after he had won the Cambridgeshire with Florence ridden by Webb?' he asked in his most truculent tones.

'I cannot swear it,' was the lame reply.

'Have you any doubt that you received this present?'

'Well, I cannot say.'

'Did it come to your knowledge that Porter complained of the way you rode that mare?'

'I should say certainly not.'

'Do you mean to say that you never heard that Porter complained of your riding?'

'He never complained to me. If he thought so why did he not come to me and say so?'

'You did not tell Porter you got this present of £500?'

'I do not know that I got it.'

That was the end of Wood as a witness of truth. It was perhaps fortunate for him that Russell did not know that he had disobeyed Porter's riding orders, which were to make all the running. Instead he had held the mare up. Had this come to Russell's attention, Wood might have suffered further humiliation.

Do what they could, however, neither Russell nor Matthews could make any progress in their efforts to connect Sir George with the villainies of Sherrard and Wood. It was in vain that Sir Henry James protested to the arbitrators that much if not all of the cross-examination of these two had nothing to do with the libel action or his client. 'This action is one thing,' he said when the cross-examinations were straying so far from the case as to border on the ridiculous, 'and the enquiry into Wood's conduct is another. I am dealing with the action before you.' But the arbitrators seemed determined to turn the hearing into a trial of the trainer and jockey and to allow a full and public disclosure of all their activities, however irrelevant to the pleadings in the case. To that end they over-ruled all Sir Henry's protests and objections. At one point a witness was called to say that he had objected to being put up by Sherrard on horses that could not win. Immediately Sir Henry protested.

'A complaint made to Wood or Sherrard cannot be evidence against Sir George Chetwynd,' he said.

Then Mr Lowther made the extraordinary admission: 'A great deal of the evidence we have had today,' he said, 'does not refer at all to Sir George Chetwynd,' and then, turning to

Russell, he said apologetically: 'I hope you will not misunderstand me, Sir Charles. A great many questions have been put concerning Wood which do not in any way affect Sir George Chetwynd.' If that was the case, why had he allowed them to be put at all?

But by this time the conduct of the enquiry had slipped from Lowther's hands and Russell was dominating it as he had dominated many stronger and more learned tribunals. When, for instance, Lord Marcus Beresford was called on behalf of Durham and asked by Russell: 'What is Wood's general reputation on the turf?' — a question which would never for a moment have been allowed in a law court — the arbitrators dismissed Sir Henry's objections and permitted it to be put in evidence.

Lord Marcus answered in the way Russell knew he would: 'With nine men out of ten Wood had the worst reputation as a jockey.' It may have been true, but it was in no way evidence against Sir George.

Several other witnesses — none of them except George Lambton, Durham's younger brother, men of any great experience in racing — were called to give evidence to the same effect. Their evidence probably should not have been admitted at all and certainly should not have carried weight with the tribunal, but it was clear that by the time Lord Durham went into the box the disclosures made by Sherrard and Wood were strongly affecting the minds of the arbitrators.

It may or may not be significant that Russell chose to call Durham last of his witnesses. It is customary for the defendant to be the first to give evidence after his case is opened. On occasion, however, if advocates feel that their client is likely to make a bad impression, they 'cover him up' by first calling other and more convincing witnesses. If this was Russell's intention — and there seems to have been little other reason for the delay in putting Durham up — he may well have been right, for Durham was by turns ignorant, arrogant, evasive and just plain rude. He displayed his prejudice and his ignorance of racing almost immediately. Answering a question about his knowledge of Wood's abilities, he said he 'rode fairly well' — this of a man who had ridden 151 winners to

1 Sir Charles Bunbury, 'the first
dictator of the Turf'
2 The Prince of Wales, later George IV
3 Sam Chifney the Elder: at his best,
he was almost unbeatable

1

3

4

5

Palmer's greatest win: leading in Goldfinder after her victory in the Chester Cup

The finish of the Gold Cup at Heaton Park Races in 1835. 'Squire' Osbaldeston's colt, Rush (owner ridden), beating Lord Wilton's Lady de Gros. From an engraving by R. G. Reeve after a painting by F. C. Turner

Lord George Bentinck, domineering, autocratic and powerful

Admiral Rous and George Payne at about the time of the Osbaldeston-Bentinck duel

6

7

8

9

10

8 The 3rd Earl of
Durham, John
George Lambton,
1855-1928
9 Sir George
Chetwynd, 4th
Bart., 1849-1917
10 John Porter, a
great trainer
11 John Porter's
yard at Kingsclere
at about the time
of the Orme
poisoning case in
1892
12 Charles Wood
was ranked second
only to Archer in
his prime

13

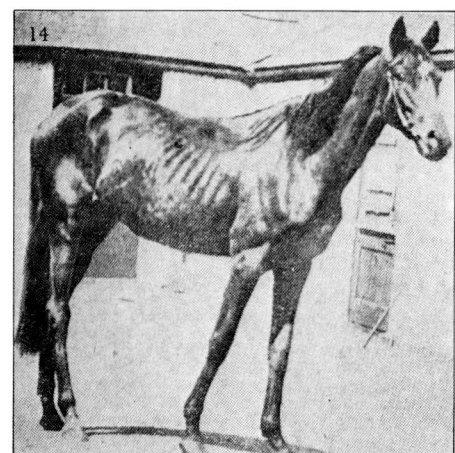

14

Nimbus
4

Sun Yat
7

Aldegond
6

Bachelor's Wedding
8

CRAGANOUR
(disq.)

GREAT SPORT
3rd

ABOYEUR
1st

LOUVOIS
2nd

MEIKLEJOHN

BENSON

KURR

DRUSCOVITCH 16

13 Emily Davidson having thrown herself in front of the King's horse, Anmer, lies dreadfully injured. Note how spectators intent on the leading horses have scarcely noticed the tragedy

14 'Before and After': this was Mr Justice Greer's comment on being handed these pictures. On the left is the real Coat of Mail; on the right, the substituted 'ringer', Jazz

15 The finish of the 1913 Derby. Note how Craganour and Aboyeur are locked together, leaning on each other, and how Day Comet, said to have been interfered with by Craganour, is on the rails well away from him and with Aboyeur between them

16 The four defendants in the Great Turf Frauds

17 Colombo going to post. Note Donoghue's silken touch on the reins, and his length of leather compared to the modern perch. At the time, his photograph was said, rightly, to illustrate the perfect racing seat

become champion jockey in 1887, the same year as the Gimcrack speech, who had won the Derby on St Blaise, and ridden St Simon in his prime.

But, in the event whatever Durham said was going to make very little difference to the outcome of the case. The allegation of malice on his part had never been put forward by Sir George's advisers. Durham's case rested on the truth or otherwise of his allegations, and these had been explored at enormous length and in great detail during the cross-examinations of Sir George, Sherrard and Wood. All Sir Henry James could do was to attempt to show that Durham might have been mistaken and that prejudice had affected his judgement. This he did with some skill and he was to a great extent successful in showing up Durham's arrogance and self-conceit as the following passages will show:

'Do you now charge Sir George Chetwynd with having committed malpractices with regard to Fullerton?' Sir Henry asked him.

'As to 1886, I do.'

'But what as to 1887?'

'No, not in 1887.' Here at least was a partial victory for Sir Henry, since the original charge had referred to 1887, and he now wanted to know why it had ever been laid and why it had not been withdrawn until this late stage.

'Did you know that these particulars were unfounded when they were delivered?' he asked. On being told that Durham did not, he pressed on. 'When did you know that these particulars were unfounded?' was his next question.

'When I went to Mr Sydney's office one day and asked to see Sir George's betting-book,' was the answer.

'Did you see it?' Sir Henry asked.

Durham could now appreciate that danger was looming ahead and he promptly became evasive. 'It was not put into my hands,' he said.

'Did you see it? Give me an answer,' Sir Henry pressed him.

Again Durham evaded the question, this time with truculence. 'I won't if you ask it in that form,' he said.

'Did you or did you not, Lord Durham, see that book?'

113

Again Durham tried to evade the question. 'Outside or inside?' he said.

'Pray answer my question —'

He was answered with more truculence from the witness: 'I won't unless you put it in a different light.'

'Now, Lord Durham, did you see that book? I am speaking to a man of intelligence?'

Here Lord March intervened to protect Durham, a course he had never taken during the cross-examinations of the plaintiff and his witnesses. 'I think', he said, 'there is some mistake between you, Sir Henry, and the witness on this point.'

'I hope there is,' was the reply, 'but I won't discuss it.' Then, turning to Durham once more, he asked: 'I am asking generally, did you see the betting-book?'

'I saw the book with reference to the races to which I wished to refer,' was the wholly unsatisfactory reply.

A little later Sir Henry asked him: 'Is it solely on the ground that the horse started twice a favourite and backed by Sir George and then wins the third time that you accuse Sir George of fraud?'

'You do not understand. You do not know much about racing,' was the arrogant answer and one which might just as well have referred to the man who made it.

A suggestion was made in cross-examination that Sherrard had told a boy, Howard, to stop Fullerton when he rode him, but, even if this were true, Russell had failed to show that Sir George was a party to it. Sir Henry now asked Durham: 'You do not suggest that Chetwynd knew of Howard's being squared by Sherrard?'

For the first time Durham hesitated and showed himself openly evasive. At length he said: 'Well, I say that he ought, from his position in the stable, to have known of it.'

This, of course, was no answer at all and Sir Henry pressed him: 'Do you say that Sir George knew of it? Yes or no?'

'I accuse him of telling either Sherrard or Wood that this horse might run at Goodwood and not win.'

Once more this had nothing to do with the question. Sir Henry was determined that he should answer it, and answer it properly: 'I ask you once more, aye or no, do you charge him?'

'How can I answer, how am I to know what Sir George Chetwynd knew? I do not even know, as a fact, that he knew that Howard was to ride the horse.' But he had already said that Sir George knew or ought to have known everything that went on in the stable. He was twisting and turning almost as badly as Wood had done. But help was at hand. Lowther intervened: 'If, Sir Henry, you will read one of Lord Durham's answers, I think it will satisfy you.'

Sir Henry, having looked at the answer in the note, promptly said it was no answer at all to the point he was on, nor indeed was it. Turning to the witness again, he put it to him once more: 'I wish to know, aye or no, Lord Durham, do you charge Sir George Chetwynd with being cognisant of Sherrard's giving instructions to the boy Howard to pull Fullerton in the Steward's Cup and the Chesterfield Cup at Goodwood in 1887?'

Whereupon Durham lost his temper. 'I do not consider you have any right to ask me that question, Sir Henry James,' he shouted, causing laughter in court. With that answer, Lowther adjourned the sitting for luncheon.

Perhaps the most preposterous and pompous answer of all came during the afternoon sitting. 'I suppose you bet at times, Lord Durham?' Sir Henry asked him.

'Oh, yes, but I am very erratic.'

'And you have had horses start though at outside prices — why?'

'I suppose because I was not backing them.'

'I see. You can be erratic but you do not give others the same privilege — not Sir George Chetwynd?'

'You see,' Durham said with typical grandiloquence, 'the public all know I am an honourable man.' This answer, not surprisingly, once more caused considerable laughter in court.

He was the last defence witness and when he left the box Russell rose to address the arbitrators on his behalf. In a typically trenchant speech he branded Chetwynd House, occupied by Sherrard and Wood, as 'a foul nest'. Sir George, he said, were he an honourable man, should have disassociated himself entirely from it: 'I can quite understand Sir George Chetwynd, if he could have afforded to do it, coming into court and,

115

knowing the broadcast aspersions resting on the name of Wood, knowing that Wood had been suspended from his career by the refusal of the Jockey Club stewards to renew his licence — I could have understood Sir George Chetwynd keeping aloof from that man; I could have understood, when coming into court, his saying: "Here I am, Sir George Chetwynd, I hold Wood at arm's length — I may have been deceived — at least I am no party to any conduct which deserves condemnation, which is not worthy of honourable men." But what was his course? His course has been deliberately to sail in the same boat with Sherrard and, up to this moment we have not heard that he had given Wood the cold shoulder. . . .'

So Sir George was to be branded because he stood by his servants. It was an argument which may have appealed to the arbitrators but was not so kindly accepted by many of the influential racing and society figures who were following the case.

When he came to the in-and-out running of Fullerton, over which he had been defeated by Sir George in cross-examination, Russell trod very carefully indeed, but on the question of the sale of horses by Wood to Chetwynd and the letter marked 'Private' he really let himself go. 'I wish to put this grave question, for on the answer you make to that as honourable gentlemen must depend practically the issue in the case though there is much else besides. If the Jockey Club had known of this transaction would they have accepted it as complying with the rules of racing? I say that Sir George Chetwynd knowingly and intentionally wrote a letter to represent one view while he wrote in a private letter — not to be shown to anyone — what was the real transaction. . . . Why was Sir George Chetwynd driven to these straits? Why, if he could not pay for these horses, did he not say so and let them be sold in the open market . . . ? They ran in Sir George's ownership in 1884, not one farthing of the price having been paid for them. So, in 1885 and 1886 up to July 5th there is nothing paid; but then a settlement was made. . . .'

Russell was, of course, right. Here was a clear breach of the rules of racing, amply proved, however Sir Henry James might attempt to explain it away by stating that the property in the horses had passed and Sir George had paid for their entries and keep from the day he assumed their ownership. Russell was also right when he admitted that this was 'practically the issue' in the case, for none of the other offences laid against him had been brought home to Sir George — so much so that in the Fullerton affair the defence had virtually abandoned the charge. It should also be pointed out that this offence, if offence it was, had been committed in 1884 — almost three years before Durham made the speech, and would never have come to light at all if Sir George had not disclosed the letter marked 'Private'.

In his reply Sir Henry dealt at great length with the charges levied against his client. He was frequently interrupted by both Lowther and Russell — Lowther constantly expressing irritation with him to such an extent that at one point the following exchange took place:

'It is no good your talking to me,' Lowther said to him, 'unless I understand what you are talking about.'

'How can you understand unless I talk to you?' was the reply. 'May I ask you to give me your attention?' It must have been obvious to him by then that the arbitrators were dead against him and he ended on a deferential note, even to the extent of apologizing for his lack of knowledge of racing. It was an admission that Russell would never have made, and cases are not won by apologies.

The arbitrators spent little time in making up their award. They found for Sir George on the question of the in-and-out running of Fullerton and other horses, awarding him a farthing damages — the same amount as the court had awarded to Wood, which may or may not have been coincidental. On the charges of having connived at serious malpractices they found for the defendant, Durham.

In plain language the verdicts meant that, although Sir George had been wronged by the allegation of cheating with his horses, his character in racing was only worth one farthing; and that he was guilty of breaches of the rules of racing so serious as to disqualify him from the rank and position in society he had hitherto enjoyed. He received the news of the result with the same impassivity and strength of character that he had

117

displayed throughout the proceedings. He was at Alexandra Park talking to Horace Lennard, a sporting journalist, when the telegram arrived. 'A farthing damages. Rather short odds,' he said, and handed the telegram to Lennard to read. Immediately afterwards he wrote to the Jockey Club tendering his resignation, believing, he said, that Lord Durham would do the same. Durham, of course, did not, and seemed determined to pursue Sir George beyond the verdict. At the next Sandown meeting Sir George, who remained a member of the National Hunt Committee, took up a position on the stewards' stand to which he had a perfect right as a member of that body. Seeing him there, Durham went to Sir Frederick Johnstone, a steward of the meeting, and demanded to know why he had allowed Sir George on to the stand. 'If you mean by that', Sir Frederick said to him, 'that you want me to turn George Chetwynd out of this stand I'll see you damned first.'

Sir George's candour in the witness box, his demeanour during the long trial and his loyalty to Sherrard and Wood had won him many friends. As has been said before, there could be no appeal and no reasons were given by the arbitrators for their decision, which seemed to many to be against the weight of much of the evidence on its true interpretation, and to be unduly harsh and unwarranted. Lennard, who had been in court throughout the entire hearing, expressed the views of a considerable section of the public and of society when he wrote:

> I wonder how many men of business in the City of London would have passed through such an ordeal as Sir George Chetwynd has done with so much credit. I do not think there are many who would care to have every action of their career, and every document connected therewith, brought into the fierce light that beats upon the witness box, during a cross-examination by Sir Charles Russell.

Durham's arrogant bearing in the witness box, too, had not gone unnoticed, nor had his underlying hostility to Sir George as displayed in his answers. When a Mr Leo Agar opened a subscription for him as a mark of esteem for his public spirit in bringing the action, few people of consequence could be persuaded to contribute. After a year, when the list was closed, it had reached the princely total of £329.

It is difficult not to arrive at the conclusion that Chetwynd was harshly treated. Much of the evidence given by Sherrard and Wood and the admissions forced from them in cross-examination had nothing at all to do with him and would not have been tolerated in a court of law. The attempts to prove his pulling of horses and his connivance with Wood in stopping them were laughable. Unquestionably the transaction disclosed in the letter marked 'Private' was a tainted one, but that alone hardly merited the draconian verdict of the arbitrators.

The whole sorry business shows Sir George to have been the victim of a personal vendetta and a witch hunt by the authorities, a state of affairs not unknown in certain racing circles before or since.

CHAPTER 6

Was Orme Poisoned?

THE ORME POISONING CASE created a sensation when it burst upon an astonished world in 1892, but it may well have been the greatest racing non-event of the century. Certainly William Allison, the special commissioner of *The Sportsman*, the most influential sporting paper of the day, thought it was and said so in no uncertain terms.

Allison was probably the first of the highly educated, literate writers to enter racing journalism and make it a full-time profession. A product of Rugby and Balliol, where he had mixed with an exclusive set and hunted and raced, he had also taken a first in law. On coming down he had been called to the bar and had founded and edited a high Tory political magazine before devoting his considerable talents to racing journalism and breeding bloodstock. He had a limpid and compelling style; he knew and loved horses, and when he did not allow his considerable prejudices to run away with him was an accurate and spirited recorder of the racing scene. He was also on terms of intimacy with some of the grander trainers and owners who admitted him further into their confidence than they did less socially acceptable members of the racing press.

Orme was a son of the mighty Ormonde, one of the greatest horses of all time, winner of the Triple Crown and unbeaten when he retired to stud as a four-year-old. A produce of his first season, Orme was out of Angelica, an unraced sister of St Simon, another immortal of the Turf. Like his sire, Orme was owned and bred by the Duke of Westminster, a Victorian magnifico who had immense success on the Turf both as an owner and as a breeder at his Eaton Hall stud in Cheshire. As a yearling Orme was sent along with others from Eaton Hall to be trained by John Porter of Kingsclere who had already won two Derbys for the Duke with Shotover and Ormonde.

Hugh Lupus, first Duke of Westminster and possibly the richest man in England at the time, was no mere figurehead as a racing magnate. An austere, reserved man and a leading member of the Jockey Club, he was a polished and expert horseman who knew as much about the owning, breeding and racing of thoroughbred racehorses as any man on the Turf and put his knowledge to good effect. He was also extremely fond of the horses he bred and raced. It was natural, therefore, that Orme, because of his famous sire, should capture the Duke's special attention and interest. And at first it looked as if Orme was destined to follow in Ormonde's footsteps. As a two-year-old he won five races, including the Middle Park Stakes, out of six starts. His only defeat was an excusable one when he finished second to Signorina in the Lancashire Plate at the Manchester September meeting when giving weight away to those others of his age who took part.

That year there was also in the stable a flying filly, La Flèche, owned by Baron de Hirsch, a friend of the Prince of Wales. La Flèche was also wonderfully successful in her two-year-old year, retiring for the winter the unbeaten winner of four races including the Champagne Stakes. Altogether the results of that season's racing fully justified the Duke writing to Porter: 'The stable is invincible. This is truly a great year for it and you. Given the material you certainly know how to make the best use of it.'

Unfortunately at the opening of the 1892 season, when Orme and La Flèche were confidently expected to carry all before them in the classics, all was not well within John Porter's stable. Porter was a great trainer; his string of successes not only in the classics but also in the big handicaps proves that. But he was a hard taskmaster and a perfectionist. Humourless and over-conscientious, he demanded a dedication equal to his own from employees and owners, not hesitating to banish either from his yard if they failed to come up to the high standards he set for them.

As it happened, he had not been noticeably successful with the horses he was then training for the Prince of Wales. Lord Marcus Beresford, the racing manager for both the Prince and Baron de Hirsch, was the opposite of Porter in almost every way. Ebullient and outgoing, Lord Marcus had a wickedly witty and at times devastatingly sarcastic tongue, which he did not hesitate to use as the whim took him, at any time and in any company, for he was no respecter of persons. A clash of temperament between the two men was almost inevitable, and Porter is said to have resented both Lord Marcus's sallies and his directives regarding the horses he managed. Certainly when the Prince's and Baron Hirsch's horses left Porter the following year and went to Richard Marsh, Porter wrote to the other trainer: 'I am glad as they are leaving me, you get them. You and I are not foolish enough to fall out with each other over other people's quarrels. . . .' And Marsh in his recollections strongly hints that there was trouble between Porter and Lord Marcus.

That there was, in addition, rivalry within the stable between the handlers of the colt and the filly and that it built up as the classics approached also appears unquestionable and is borne out by all the chroniclers of the times. It spread, too, to the public; interest and excitement increased and every scrap of news concerning their comings and goings was awaited with eagerness and avidly seized upon. This was especially so in the case of Orme who, it was hoped, might well surpass the achievements of his mighty sire.

Orme was not given a preparatory race before the Two Thousand Guineas. He satisfied Porter in his work and all seemed well, except that the Duke fell ill and was confined to bed. It was nothing serious, Porter was informed, but it was unlikely that the Duke would be able to attend Newmarket and have the pleasure of seeing his colt, as everyone confidently expected, carry off the first classic.

On the Friday before the race Lord Marcus Beresford, accompanied by Prince Adolphus of Teck and a Mr Portal, visited Porter who took them round the yard. When they came to the 'Derby winner's' box which Orme occupied, and where Common and Sainfoin had been stabled before him, Porter noticed saliva dripping from the colt's mouth. At first he was not unduly concerned, for Orme had a habit of trying to bite the metal strips on the walls of his box and because of that always wore a muzzle when at rest. He also had a way of putting his tongue outside his mouth and chafing it, causing foam to form.

Nevertheless, as soon as the visitors had left Porter hurried back to Orme's box and examined his mouth. He found it swollen and tender to the touch, the running from the mouth had increased and blisters were beginning to form under the tongue. Porter's immediate reaction was to conclude that the trouble sprang from Orme's teeth. He sent a telegram to Loeffler, the famous German horse dentist who was in practice at Newmarket, requesting him to come to Kingsclere as soon as he could. As an added precaution, in case the colt should be developing a cough, he rubbed his throat with mustard and moved him to a more isolated box for fear of infection. At this time it appears that no thought of poisoning crossed his mind.

Loeffler arrived the following morning and examined Orme's mouth. Loeffler possessed an almost hypnotic power over horses which enabled him to treat the most savage and intractable animal without narcotics or sedatives. He was a brilliant man but he was also opinionated, dogmatic and highly-strung to the point of eccentricity. His diagnosis was that one of the molars was decayed and that this was the seat of the trouble. Since it was the time that the shedding of a molar could be expected, he advised extraction. Porter agreed and, according to him — for, as will be seen, here Porter's and Loeffler's accounts differ — Loeffler then extracted the tooth. The two men examined the tooth; both agreed that there was a highly offensive smell coming from it. According to Porter Loeffler said that the tooth was septic and that nothing else was wrong with the horse. Porter disagreed and said there must be something more and that the smell was caused by pieces of decaying food adhering to

123

the tooth. The argument became heated and Loeffler left. He went straight on to Welbeck where he had an appointment to treat one of the Duke of Portland's horses. He told Portland what had happened and what his opinion was.

It was noon by the time Loeffler left and Orme, of course, had not been out with the string. Porter hated touts and touting. He had been known to deal out draconian justice to those whom he caught, but with Orme and La Flèche on his hands there were bound to be observers and nothing he did could stop some of them watching his horses work. Immediately Orme's absence was spotted. 'Orme I did not see out' was one message wired to the press.

No statement about the horse or explanation for his non-appearance at work was issued from Kingsclere. Over the weekend the wildest rumours began to fly about London. Nor, despite the strict precautions Porter took to ensure security among his stable lads, could he entirely prevent unauthorised information leaving his yard.

He said afterwards that he had discovered that one of his lads on his day off had hired a horse and ridden into Newbury to tell friends that Orme would not run in the Derby. At the same time this lad must have conveyed to those friends something of the nature of Orme's setback. Instantly stories of foul play began to proliferate.

On Sunday Orme was no better and Porter sent for Mr Williams, his vet. Williams and his son came over and examined the horse. The tongue was still swollen and the blisters had increased in size, but there was no running from the nose and the temperature was normal. Williams lanced the blisters and drew off the fluid. There were no overt signs of poisoning and Williams, though he entertained the possibility of it, did not then think it a likely prognosis. He confessed himself puzzled by the symptoms and how to diagnose them. Neither he nor Porter considered or suggested sending samples of saliva or the fluid from the blisters for analysis, nor were antidotes of any sort administered.

Much later, when he had changed his tune over the whole matter, Porter endeavoured to explain this away by saying that an attempt had been made to poison Orme by giving him a ball saturated in mercury. Since Orme was a difficult swallower the ball had not gone beyond his mouth, which explained the irritation set up there and the absence of other bodily symptoms. It is significant, however, that at the time he did not think it necessary to inform the Duke of Westminster of the colt's illness and in fact, on the next day, Monday, Orme was better and taking soft food.

It was on the Monday, however, that the real storm broke in the public prints. Every one of them carried on their sporting pages headlines reporting Orme's illness and most hinted strongly at his having been got at. Worse still, hordes of reporters began to descend on Kingsclere.

Porter was then in a quandary. The Duke of Westminster was a very great grandee; he was Porter's most important owner; Orme was the hottest Derby favourite for years. What were the Duke's reactions likely to be when he read these stories suggesting that Orme had been poisoned when no news of any such event had been conveyed to him by the trainer?

Early on Tuesday morning Porter sent a telegram to the Duke, briefly outlining what had happened and telling him that he was immediately despatching Williams to Eaton Hall with a full explanation. Williams did not reach Eaton until late that night, and in the meantime the excitement in the press continued unabated. It even spread to America and several leading New York journalists including a Mrs Elizabeth A. Tomkins, one of the first of the sob-sisters, were sent over to cover it.

Porter himself remained silent and refused to issue any statement or to give any interviews. But news drifted out, as it always does from a racing stable, and the leaks may have been assisted by the rifts within the stable itself. At any rate, word got about that Orme was not as bad as had first been suggested, that he had begun to recover immediately after the blisters had been lanced and was, in fact, already being walked out. In consequence a sceptical note began to appear in certain papers. To the great annoyance of Porter this piece of facetiousness was printed in *Punch*: 'Orme! Sweet Orme! Orme is still off solid food and is kept alive entirely by Porter. It is the opinion of the best informed that "Porter with a head on" will pull him through. . . .'

No one knows what passed between the Duke and Williams at their interview, but in view of the hullabaloo in the press and the veiled suggestions that Orme was not as bad as he had been made out to be it would not be unnatural for Williams to have propounded the poisoning theory, perhaps unduly. Porter later recorded that he had told Williams to explain 'that we had no doubt that an attempt had been made to poison the horse although we had no actual proof of it'.

The Duke, who was still indisposed and perhaps not able to weigh up the facts as clearly as he might have been, appears to have at once accepted as a fact and without further evidence that a wicked attempt had been made to poison the best classic prospect he had had since Ormonde. In an attempt to silence the sceptics and to bring to justice the perpetrators of the outrage he issued the following notice for publication:

ONE THOUSAND POUNDS REWARD — POISONING OF ORME. Whereas, on the 21st of April last, at Kingsclere Stable, in the County of Hants, the racehorse Orme, the property of his Grace the Duke of Westminster, was wilfully poisoned, the above reward will be paid by the Duke of Westminster to any person who shall, within one month from this date, furnish such information as shall lead to the apprehension and conviction of the person or persons guilty of the said crime. Information should be furnished to Messrs Lewis & Lewis, Ely Place, Holborn, E.C.

The publication of this notice brought no immediate result except that press comment became increasingly suspicious and cynical. Shortly afterwards the Duke seems to have had second thoughts for on 29 April he sent the following letter to *The Sportsman* — William Allison's paper.

SIR,
Orme is better but was nearly dead on Sunday and

126

Monday, and was only kept alive by injections of milk and eggs. It is hoped that he may recover sufficiently to meet his Derby engagement. I am afraid there can be no doubt that a very virulent poison was administered to him, probably twice — on Thursday and Friday in last week.

I remain, sir,

yours obediently,

WESTMINSTER.

If Porter's later statements are to be accepted this letter is an extraordinary one, for even when the Duke was writing it Orme was, according to Porter, 'hovering between life and death'.

At the same time the Duke also sent a message to *The Sportsman* that he would like William Allison to go to Kingsclere, interview Porter and report on just what was going on there. It was a tribute to Allison's standing in high quarters that the Duke should have singled him out for such a mission. As it happened it was inconvenient for him to travel to Kingsclere on that day owing to social engagements, but he could scarcely ignore such a summons and he went. When sending the Duke's message to Allison the staff of *The Sportsman* omitted to convey to him the contents of the letter which would probably be published on the same day as Allison's report of his visit to Kingsclere.

When he arrived Allison had a glimpse of Orme being walked into his box. Brief though the opportunity for inspection was, to his experienced eye the colt looked well enough in himself and in no way answered to Porter's later description of how all the hairs in his coat were falling out, and his skin looking 'as though it had been shaved with a razor'. In fact, after asking if he could see him in his box and being told that no one from outside the stable would be allowed into it, he commented to Porter: 'He does not look so bad after all, Mr Porter,' and Porter agreed, saying that he was picking up nicely.

The two men were on friendly terms and Porter opened his heart to Allison. He was, he said, at a loss to know just what had happened. It could be poisoning, though he was now inclined to discount that theory. It could be the tooth, though he disputed that too. The trouble might, in fact, have come from a multitude of causes none of which, it seemed, could be accurately diagnosed. But — the colt was recovering. 'Williams,' he said, 'though, like me, he was suspicious, would not stake his reputation that the horse had been poisoned.' At all events he was now on the mend, and he might well run in the Derby.

'But, Mr Porter, he nearly died on Sunday, did he not?' Allison asked.

'Died? Not a bit of it,' was Porter's reply.

Porter was under very considerable pressure and may have spoken more freely to Allison than he intended. He was certainly incautious when he indicated to him that the Duke might have been too hasty in rushing into print with the flat statement that Orme had been poisoned. Allison must have realized this, for before he left he asked Porter if he could publish all that had passed between them, pointing out that it could well cause trouble with the Duke if what he printed contained a contradiction of the Duke's statement. Notwithstanding this, Porter gave him permission to print all he had said. It is exceedingly hard to understand why he gave this authority, which, had he paused to consider, he must have known would upset the Duke. One can only assume that the pressures he was under from within the stable and from outside were so great that he acted irrationally and without thinking. At all events later, even under professional advice, he never denied that he had given Allison all-embracing permission to publish. It must be remembered, too, that at that time he still hoped to run the colt in the Derby and, with that in mind, he may well have wanted to play down the effects of his illness.

Again, too, Porter must have been fully aware of the rivalries and discontent within the stable. Stories of poisoning reflected on the staff and were likely to heighten an already charged atmosphere. This may have been another reason for his wish to throw at least some cold water on the widely exaggerated reports of the colt's illness and its symptoms which were now circulating everywhere. If these, or any of them, were his motives they were mistaken. What he told Allison only made matters far worse.

During the drive to Newbury from Kingsclere and going back in the train Allison wrote up his notes. While he did so he pondered the whole matter. He became convinced that Orme had not been poisoned at all. His conclusion was that Orme's symptoms were caused by the condition of his teeth. He himself had observed on other occasions Orme's habit of moving his tongue in and out of his mouth and creating a mass of foam. From this, in his own words, he propounded the theory: 'Is it not conceivable that he may have, while doing this, scratched his tongue on that decayed tooth, and that the decayed matter, acting as an irritant, should have set up the local inflammation, blisters, etc?' He wrote this into his report, telegraphed it to *The Sportsman* and went home to entertain his friends to dinner.

Next morning when he opened his copy of *The Sportsman* he found the Duke's letter alongside his report and then, to use his own words, 'I knew there would be ructions.'

To protect himself from those ructions he immediately set off for Newmarket to interview Loeffler, whom he hoped would confirm his theory. Loeffler did that and more. 'Would it surprise you to know', were Loeffler's first words to him, 'that the tooth I am supposed to have extracted is still in his head?'

This startling statement rather took Allison's breath away but Loeffler went on to explain that the tooth which was causing the trouble was a back one which was not due to shed until next year. The first tooth, of which he had only been able to take away a small part, was in pieces and the one underneath, coming up, was badly decayed. 'There is nothing more mysterious about the illness', Loeffler flatly declared, 'than a man with a decayed tooth having a faceache.' The excess of saliva, he went on to say, was a natural result of the swollen tongue which, together with the blisters, had been caused by contact with the sharp edges of the broken tooth — 'and thus becoming inoculated, so to speak, with decayed matter. There is poison enough in that. If you knew what that tooth smells like you — oh, you would *never* forget it.'

'May I take it, then, Mr Loeffler, that in your opinion Orme was not poisoned?'

'Undoubtedly you may.'

Reassured, Allison returned to town but that, as he had guessed, was far from being the end of the matter. The Duke was furious. Having recovered from his illness he travelled to London, pursued by reporters all the way, and installed himself in Grosvenor House. This alone would have been enough to upset his austere and publicity-hating temperament. He summoned Porter to his presence and gave him a dressing-down, the details of which Porter never disclosed. George Lewis, the great Victorian society solicitor, was also present at the interview. It was Lewis whom the Duke had instructed to disclose the information about the supposed poisoning. Porter had to make a full statement of the facts to him and a letter was drafted to *The Sportsman* correcting and amending as best as could be Allison's article. Lewis was also instructed to employ a private detective, and Inspector Buckler of Scotland Yard was called in.

Despite all Lewis's skills in drafting, Porter's letter was singularly unconvincing. It could scarcely be otherwise since Allison had gone to Kingsclere at the Duke's request, his *bona fides* as the leading racing reporter of the day could not be challenged — at least not without the grave risk of a libel action — and, similarly, the letter could not and did not attempt to deny that Porter had given him permission to publish.

Allison made a courteous and devastating reply, totally demolishing the letter and stressing that Porter had instructed him 'to hold back nothing'. No further response came from either Porter or the Duke, but the letters unleashed a positive whirlwind of correspondence. Vets, amateur and professional, dentists — horse and human, wits, gamblers, trainers, almost everyone who could hold a pen or an opinion rushed into print. Most of the letters, it must be said, were scathing about Porter, the Duke and George Lewis, though Loeffler came in for his share of criticism too. Most unwisely he took issue with certain of the correspondents and defended himself in detail with lengthy letters. One at least of the wits was, however, on his side:

Mr George Lewis, who is reported to have ridiculed Professor Loeffler's views on the subject of Orme's decayed tooth, may or may not be an eminent horse dentist. I always understood him to be a lawyer, but, of course, I may be mistaken. Possibly in the confusion of this case we shall presently find Professor Loeffler ridiculing Mr George Lewis on a point of law.

Unfortunately Loeffler never had the chance of ridiculing George Lewis on a point of law or anything else. The worry and stress of the whole affair so affected his health that he had a nervous breakdown and had to be confined to an institution.

Despite the activity and the publicity, despite the offer of a £1,000 reward, despite the activities of the detective, no evidence was unearthed to substantiate the poisoning theory or to reveal the identity of the alleged poisoner or poisoners, nor were they ever brought to justice.

In his memoirs Porter states that he was all but sure the culprit was one of his stable lads, but that he was never able to establish his guilt. It has been said — but not by Porter — that he brought this lad, together with another whom he suspected, before George Lewis. In spite of a devastating cross-examination by the great lawyer no admission or confession was obtained. If Porter really knew the identity of the culprit it seems inconceivable that the combined efforts of himself, the Duke, Inspector Buckler and George Lewis could not have brought his guilt home to him. Porter goes on to say: 'Since the case against him was not conclusive in a legal sense, I could do no more than discharge him.'

Dismissal on pure suspicion scarcely accords with justice, natural or otherwise, and may go some way towards explaining the discontent in Porter's stable. At this time Porter was above all concerned to rehabilitate himself in the eyes of the Duke. One can hardly blame him, for the Duke was his most prestigious owner and wielded enormous power in the racing world. Matters were already not going well between Porter and Lord Marcus; to lose Westminster's horses and his influence as well as those of the Prince of Wales and Baron de Hirsch in one year would be a total disaster. At all events Porter, after his interview with the Duke, and having adopted the poisoning theory, devoted all his efforts to substantiating it. In both his books of memoirs he roundly asserts that Orme was the victim of an outrage. In the earlier work he states: 'In the course of a fortnight the hair came off in patches, and for a period of ten days the horse's life was despaired of. He was so weak he could scarcely stand without assistance.' This is a direct contradiction of what he told Allison and indeed of what Allison himself saw — and Allison, it must be remembered, visited the stable within a week of the discovery of the symptoms. In his later book Porter slightly modifies the earlier account, saying: 'For several days Orme hovered between life and death. It was almost a hopeless case. . . .'

Along with many others Allison did not for a moment accept Porter's denials or the Duke's statements. But when Porter came to him and told him he was in the Duke's bad books over Allison's article he very sportingly said: 'Blame my memory. Don't on any account let me cause trouble.'

Allison, however, never wavered from the belief that Orme had not been poisoned and he refused to retract. He was also firmly of the opinion that the whole affair had been blown up into the sensation it was by the Duke's too hasty assumption of poisoning without waiting for proof, and his rushing out the notice offering a reward. There was little he could do about it without injuring Porter further, but he had a gift for pastiche and he wrote what he called a 'burlesque' entitled *The Duchess of Pimlico's Cat, or Poison Proved (A society Dramatette)*, which he submitted anonymously to a rival paper, *The Sporting Times*. It contained in its *dramatis personae*, as well as the Duchess herself, Tom, her cat, Mr Muffler, a chiropodist, and Mr George, a solicitor. It opened with 'Tom, the cat, discovered in convulsions' and went on to guy in the broadest terms the Duchess's haste in presuming her pet to be poisoned. The allusions were obvious and were lost on no one, least of all the Duke and Porter. It was perhaps fortunate for Allison that neither of them ever discovered its authorship, though Porter refers to it in disparaging terms in his first book.

It is, in fact, a marked tribute to the esteem in which Allison was held amongst the racing great that, despite their differences and all that he had said about Orme's alleged poisoning, he was the only journalist invited to Kingsclere along with the Duke, Lord Marcus and Sir George Maude, the breeder of La Flèche, to watch Orme and La Flèche put through their final work-out prior to the St Leger.

Before that, however, Orme was not thought sufficiently recovered to run in the Derby. The other representative from Porter's stable, the filly, La Flèche did, and started favourite at 2—1 on. Ridden abominably by George Barrett she was beaten three parts of a length by the unconsidered outsider Sir Hugo. The only immediate interest of the race to this account is that the supporters of Orme in the Kingsclere stable openly and vociferously expressed their delight in La Flèche's defeat.

If Orme had in fact been poisoned and was as ill as Porter said he was then he had a wonderful constitution. By mid-June he was back in strong work and in July won the Eclipse Stakes, giving a splendid exhibition of gameness and determination to beat Orvieto by a neck. At Goodwood a fortnight later he had another hard race in the Sussex Stakes, just getting home from a stable companion, Baron de Hirsch's Watercress, whom Porter had not expected to run and only did so on his owner's and Lord Marcus's insistence.

Orme was then prepared for the St Leger, in which he was unplaced. George Barrett's riding was blamed for this defeat. Before the race rumours spread that the bookies had bought Barrett, and the Duke, again acting on rumour and jumping to conclusions, went to Barrett and warned him that he would be kept under close surveillance from the moment he mounted the horse. Barrett had an unstable temperament — he subsequently went off his head — and this warning unnerved him. Determined to show that it was undeserved, he rode Orme in the worst possible way, dashing him to the front early on and riding him into the ground. The Duke's hasty action was unfortunate, for beforehand Barrett was confident of winning. 'He made Watercress fairly faint out of it in that last strong mile and three-quarters gallop,' he told Allison the day before the race.

After the St Leger Orme was not given much rest. Brought to Newmarket, he won in succession the Great Foal Stakes, the Champion Stakes and the Subscription Stakes. The day after the Subscription Stakes he was started in the Free Handicap of ten furlongs, in which he failed by a length and a half to give El Diabolo 16lb. Porter's comment on this defeat was: 'As this was his third race in three days he may have been a little stale.' — this of a horse whose life had been despaired of a bare four months before! Orme was then retired for the season and his subsequent history has no part to play in this account save to say that the poisoning, if poisoning it was, did not affect his four-year-old career. He ran four times in the following season winning three of his races including the Eclipse for the second time and the Gordon Stakes at Goodwood, beating La Flèche in each of them. Owing to suspensory trouble incurred in his last race he was retired to stud at the end of the season.

Was he poisoned? Most racing writers, following Porter's categorical statements in two books and the ducal statement from Eaton Hall, have accepted the poisoning as a fact. Allison says that the Duke's influence was so great that few cared to oppose him in any way, and so 'he succeeded in imposing his opinion on the general public.' He certainly imposed it on Porter in no mean fashion. Edward Moorhouse, who ghosted Porter's second volume of memoirs, appears to have toned down the poisoning account to some extent and in his history of the Derby he comments that the mystery surrounding Orme's illness was never satisfactorily solved, despite the offer of £1,000.

In opposition to the generally accepted theory, all the evidence points to Orme not having been poisoned and to Allison and Loeffler being correct. Porter's first interview with Allison, whose account of it was never materially challenged, played down the idea of poisoning and it was not until after his stormy session with the Duke that he changed his tune and backed the poisoning theory to the hilt.

The offer of a £1,000 reward was enormous in those days and it is unlikely, especially given the discontent and rivalries within Porter's stable, that, had the poison been administered by one of the lads, one or other of them would not have split on him to claim the reward. Porter's statement in old age that he knew the culprit but could not prove it scarcely holds water either, given the forces of power and privilege ranged against the suspect. It must be remembered, too, that no saliva or other tests were made to determine the presence of poison, no antidote was administered and, perhaps most significant of all, there was no sudden or inspired fielding against the horse in the betting which would have been expected had bookmakers or heavy gamblers, the only persons likely to benefit by his illness, been behind the matter.

There is one possibility which would justify the poisoning theory, though it is a remote one; it stems from the intense rivalry in the stable between the supporters of Orme and those of La Flèche. Could one of the lads in the La Flèche faction, acting entirely on his own, have obtained a mercury 'ball' and endeavoured unsuccessfully to administer it? If he failed to get the ball down Orme's throat it would have had a strongly irritant effect on the colt's mouth. Being terrified he might not have disclosed his intentions and their result to anyone. It is a possibility but a most unlikely one. And even Porter was never able to suggest a motive for the crime he alleged to have been committed. It was he himself who told Allison that there was no rush to lay against the horse before the news broke, such as he would have expected had the illness come from a deliberate act.

Everything points to Allison's theory being correct — there was never any poisoning and the whole storm in a teacup blew up through the Duke acting too hastily and then, being the man he was in the position he was, refusing to withdraw. After all, he compounded his errors by that too-hasty confrontation with Barrett which even Porter admits probably cost them the St Leger.

The Duke of Portland who was a steward of the Jockey Club about that time, writing much later wholeheartedly endorses Loeffler's opinion. 'I myself', he wrote, 'thought (and still think) it (the tooth) the most likely cause of the trouble about which all sorts of exaggerated and foolish reports were current.' It is significant, too, that so good a judge as George Lambton discounted the poisoning theory in its entirety and ascribed the illness to wrong diagnosis and treatment by Williams and his son.

But one wonders what happened to the unfortunate stable lad

who was dismissed on suspicion and no doubt without a reference — a tiny victim of Victorian privilege and autocracy.

Perhaps the strangest sequel to the whole affair was that when Orme retired to stud almost the first to receive from the Duke a nomination to him for one of his mares was William Allison.

CHAPTER 7

The Great Turf Frauds

WHAT CAME TO BE KNOWN as The Great Turf Frauds or the de Goncourt affair sprang from the fertile brain of William Kurr, a man who had previously existed by setting up a number of fly-by-night betting agencies, many of them operating under grandiloquent names, whose sole object was, to use his own words, 'to advise people to back horses which did not have a chance'.

Kurr was most ably assisted by Henry Benson, a confidence man and rogue of many aliases who was branded, not unjustly, by one of the counsel at the subsequent trial as 'exquisite in vice and excellent in fraud'. Benson from time to time posed with great success as a French nobleman incognito. He may even have come to believe in his second and separate existence himself, for he had his handkerchiefs made with a coronet in one corner over the letter M, 'Montagu' being the most favoured of his fictitious titles. It was in fact this 'French connection' which set the whole fraud off and almost enabled its perpetrators to get clean away with it.

Kurr, who was twenty-six at the time of the frauds, had started as a clerk in a railway company. At the age of fifteen, being bored, he ran away and endeavoured to make a living backing horses. By hanging around racing stables and race-courses he got a thorough education in the seamier side of racing, but the venture yielded no financial profit. He next secured a position with a money-lender in Brook Street. The business was almost certainly shady and it closed six months after Kurr had joined it. He then returned to racing but his experiences had taught him not to continue to bet on his own account and with his own money. From what he had seen in the money-lender's office he had learnt something of the general gullibility of mankind and he set up the first of his fraudulent betting agencies, aimed, as he candidly admitted, at 'plundering and swindling the public'.

Kurr's system was a simple one. He would open a betting or 'investment' agency, and advertise that he was an expert in picking winners, giving fictitious examples of his successes. When the money came in he either did not place a bet at all or, on the rare occasions when he did, would put a small portion on a runner he was convinced had no chance. When things began to get too hot for him he would close down the agency, make off with the funds, lie low for a while and then open up under another name.

Soon it became obvious that police were on his tracks, but Kurr was not one to let this deter him. In April 1882 he arranged a meeting in the Angel Public House, Islington, with Detective-Sergeant John Meiklejohn, a plain clothes man in charge of most of the investigations into illegal betting and racing transactions. In the course of his work Meiklejohn had to associate with unsavoury characters of all sorts. He was fond of money, he was much exposed to temptation, and early in his career he had yielded to it. For some years he had been known to the underworld as a corrupt police officer. Meiklejohn now suggested that Kurr might help him by giving information, and in return he would 'look after' Kurr. This was agreed; Meiklejohn handed Kurr one of his cards and arranged where contact could be made. A little later, when the net looked like closing round Kurr, Meiklejohn tipped him off and Kurr took ship for America where he remained for six months. For this service Meiklejohn received £100 from Kurr.

Immediately on his return Kurr again arranged a meeting with Meiklejohn. He now had more ambitious plans formulated during his stay abroad — he intended to set up an agency on a larger scale and to extend his operations to France. For this he required police protection, which Meiklejohn was prepared to give him — at a price. To raise the necessary capital for his larger venture Kurr resumed his practice of operating small fly-by-night agencies in which, with Meiklejohn keeping a watchful eye on warrants about to be issued ('I can settle that affair for you in Scotland for £100,' he wrote on one occasion), he was successful. Kurr actually went to Scotland Yard himself from time to time to pay Meiklejohn off, but when this became too risky they met in public houses.

Satisfied that he was safe from interference by the police and by then possessed of sufficient capital, in 1875 Kurr decided to press ahead with his more ambitious scheme. But since much of this was to be carried out in France and his knowledge of French was only rudimentary, he had to have assistance. By chance when reading a newspaper his eye fell upon an advertisement stating that a young man, an excellent linguist able to translate into many languages and write articles for newspapers on many subjects, was looking for employment of a literary character. Kurr answered the advertisement and Henry Benson, then aged twenty-seven, presented himself for an interview.

The son of a substantial merchant who carried on business partly in France and partly in England, Benson had been educated in both countries. He spoke French like a native and was also fluent in Spanish and Italian. He was also an able and convincing writer in all three languages. At the outbreak of the Franco-Prussian War he was in Brussels earning a living of a sort by freelance writing and gambling. As the war progressed he let it be known that Benson was not in fact his name at all. In reality he was the Comte de Montégut, son of a General of Division, and secretly engaged in a delicate diplomatic mission between the governments of the two countries. This explanation was accepted without question and he mixed in the best circles of Brussels society. At the end of the war he left for England, leaving the impression behind him that his journey was concerned with conducting negotiations of the highest importance involving the London government. What in fact he was about to do was to perpetrate a most gigantic fraud. In the guise of the Comte de Montégut, carrying with him two letters of introduction bearing the forged signatures of well-known names, he presented himself to the Lord Mayor of London. He was, he said, the 'mendicant envoy' of the citizens of the town of Châteaudun which had suffered terribly during the war. As a result, so he told the Lord Mayor, people were starving and actually dying in the streets. Succour, he said, was most urgently needed. The Lord Mayor had under his control a substantial fund subscribed from all over the country for the relief of the distressed people of France. Convinced by the 'Comte' and without further investigation or enquiry, he presented him with a cheque for £50,000 and a letter of sympathy from the citizens of London to the distressed and unfortunate inhabitants of Châteaudun. Benson returned to Brussels and embarked on a riotous career of extravagance and dissipation, setting himself up in true aristocratic style with a mansion, carriages and servants and entertaining on the grand scale. Soon, however, when no word came from Châteaudun as to the receipt of the cheque, the Lord Mayor's suspicions were aroused. Scotland Yard was called in, Benson was traced, arrested, tried and sentenced to a year in Newgate. While there he attempted to commit suicide by setting fire to his bed. A warder saved his life but he suffered such severe injuries that he became a cripple.

Kurr and Benson appear immediately to have recognized the other for what he was — a successful, convincing and audacious crook. They went into partnership under the name and style of Archer & Co., The Systematic Investment Society — and they prospered. Much of their business was carried on in France and this of course was entrusted to Benson who drafted the advertisements that appeared in French papers and answered the correspondence from France. It was he, too, who issued the spurious cheques to clients for their imaginary gains. This went on for some time to the great profit of Kurr and Benson until at length certain French banks began to take an interest in these cheques for substantial sums which transpired to be not only valueless but to be drawn on accounts that did not exist. Investigations were once more set on foot; once again Scotland Yard was called in, and the case was placed in the hands of Chief Inspector Nathaniel Druscovitch.

Though of Slav extraction, Druscovitch was English-born and an English citizen. He was a fluent French- and Italian-speaker and this, combined with his 'intelligence and meritorious conduct' which had won him among other commendations a special letter from the Tsar of Russia, had earned him rapid promotion in the force. He was only thirty-six when put in charge of the Yard's Foreign Bureau.

Druscovitch was soon on the track of Benson and Kurr though at the time he did not know just whom he was after, for the two principals had taken the precaution of setting up two front men, Walters and Murray, as the apparent proprietors of Archer & Co. But Meiklejohn knew and the moment he learnt that Druscovitch was about to move he wrote to Kurr:

> Dear Bill,
> Rather important news from the North. Tell H.S. and the young one to keep themselves quiet. In the event of a smell stronger than now they must be ready to scamper out of the way. I should like to see you as early as possible. In any circumstances the 'brief' [i.e. warrant] is out. If not, it will be so you must keep a sharp look out.

Archer & Co. was promptly closed down and the two chief partners, having cleared about £20,000 (about £2 million today) between them, retired for the moment to live a life of affluence. Kurr purchased a couple of racehorses, aptly named Chance and Coroner, and began to cut a dash on the Turf. Benson, assuming on this occasion the name of Yonge, repaired to the Isle of Wight where he took a lease of a villa at Shanklin called Rose Cottage and resumed his aristocratic way of life. Installing himself with a housekeeper, butler, footman and valet, two coachmen and several carriages, he let it be known that, although he adopted the name of Yonge, he was in fact a French nobleman incognito and his real name and style was that of the Comte de Montagu. Benson was a well-spoken, well-educated and convincing rogue. Almost immediately he was accepted into the best society on the island. When the Empress of Austria visited the Isle of Wight on her first sporting tour in

1875 he actually called on her as the Comte de Montagu and was received. In the following year, when she was in Northamptonshire hunting with the Pytchley, a deputation of the most important people in the island waited on him to ask if he would write to her requesting the honour of a return visit. This he did and received in reply the following letter from the Austrian Ambassador:

Sir — in answer to the request sent by you in the name of the inhabitants of Shanklin to Her Majesty the Empress Queen I am authorized to inform you that Her Majesty, while exceedingly touched by the sentiments of sympathy for her august person which have inspired your request, has not been able to give her patronage to what you ask. Accept, sir, the assurance of my distinguished consideration.

BEUST.

During his stay on the island Benson made frequent trips abroad staying at the best hotels in Paris and Biarritz, sometimes under the style of the Comte de Montagu or Montégut — the titles appeared interchangeable — at others as the Marquis de Montgomery and, even more grandiloquently, Prince Murat. On occasions, he was accompanied by Kurr who travelled under the name of Captain Gifford. It was believed that the trips were connected with further swindles that were never brought home to them. An attempt, however, to float the 'City of Paris Loan' never really got off the ground, apparently because Druscovitch intercepted the letters of request for funds and Benson, following a tip-off from Meiklejohn, hurriedly had to close the operation down. This did not, however, stop him leading a double life in London as well as abroad for, along with Kurr, he turned once more to racing frauds. Together they set up the Society for Insurance Against Losses on the Turf, for which they took offices in Moorgate Street and Gresham Street.

For a little while this entirely bogus venture flourished, but someone at the Yard was now alert to their activities though the identities of the principals was not known. Warrants were issued against the front men, Walters and Murray, who were arrested. Meiklejohn once more proved his worth to Kurr and Benson by letting them know what was afoot. Immediately they disappeared again into their respective identities of pillar of the Turf and doyen of Isle of Wight society. Walters and Murray were allowed bail so Kurr, realizing that awkward disclosures might be made should they come to trial, put them in funds to abscond and they made a hurried departure to America.

All this, combined with their lifestyles, cost money, and by the middle of 1876 both Kurr and Benson were beginning to run short of cash. Together they began to hatch their most audacious fraud. It was to be carried out entirely in France which would, they thought, ensure their safety from detection. They procured a French directory which Benson went through, concentrating on the districts of the Marne and Garonne and selecting names of those whom he thought likely subjects for the receipt of their circulars. Most of the names came, he said afterwards, from the ranks of 'notaries and gentry'. To back up the supposed authenticity of these circulars they proposed to publish an entirely bogus racing newspaper to be composed by themselves and translated into French by Benson, under the title *Le Sport*.

Once they had decided to go ahead it was obviously necessary to protect themselves against interference by the police. The invaluable Meiklejohn was therefore called in and the scheme explained to him. Although he said he could not fully understand it he was prepared to co-operate so far as he was able, but he added that he could not by himself guarantee immunity. If there was any stink kicked up in France, he said, Druscovitch would almost certainly handle the investigation and Druscovitch was, so far as he knew, incorruptible and a difficult man to approach.

There, for a little while, the matter rested. And then the conspirators had an astonishing piece of luck. Druscovitch's brother ran into financial trouble in the shape of a bill for £60 which he could not meet. He was threatened with having the Sherriff's men put in and, in desperate straits, he came to Druscovitch looking for a loan. Druscovitch himself was short of funds and had not got £60 to lend him. He in turn went to Meiklejohn, who instantly saw his chance and seized it. He could not lend the money, he said, but he knew someone who would. When Druscovitch asked who the friend was Meiklejohn told him: 'He is a perfect gentleman, an owner of racehorses whom you may thoroughly trust.' He was, of course, none other than William Kurr. Druscovitch still hesitated, but the brother's needs were pressing and eventually he agreed to a meeting at the Pentonville Arms, a public house which Kurr and Meiklejohn used for their transactions. At this meeting Kurr handed the detective £60 in £10 notes.

Although Druscovitch had now received this money Meiklejohn warned both Kurr and Benson that it was by no means sufficient to suborn him, and that it might well be paid back very soon which would render the whole transaction completely innocent. He did know, however, that Druscovitch was continually financing his brother who was an improvident spendthrift and that therefore he was constantly short of ready cash. Kurr, Benson and Meiklejohn had frequent discussions as to how Druscovitch could be squared. Finally Meiklejohn was entrusted with the task of insinuating himself into Druscovitch's confidence and gradually suggesting to him that there were means available by which his financial difficulties could be overcome. He did this with considerable success and at the beginning of August he was satisfied that the trap was ready to be sprung. Accordingly he wrote to Kurr:

> Dear Bill,
> I have written to Dustman [their code name for Druscovitch] saying I had a letter from you this morning, and asking you to meet him at the Swan public house Clapham Road, at 8 p.m. this day, Monday, so you know how things stand.

The meeting took place. Kurr told Druscovitch that he wanted to help him and would, in return, require some services, but he did not tell him the truth. He maintained that all they proposed to do was to open a betting office. At that time, as Kurr of course knew, there was considerable sympathy in the Force with those who evaded the rules against off-the-course betting. It was regarded as a venial crime and indeed those who committed it often assisted the police with valuable information gleaned from their criminal contacts. All they would require, Kurr said, was a tip-off if there was trouble coming from a higher source than Meiklejohn could handle. Still Druscovitch hesitated. Then Kurr took the plunge and handed him £25 in sovereigns. At first Druscovitch refused to accept them, saying: 'I can't take that, you have lent me £60 already.' 'That's of no consequence,' was Kurr's reply, and he pushed the money into Druscovitch's pocket.

Druscovitch walked away with the gold still in his possession. He kept it and spent it and by so doing effectively put an end to a police career which was already emerging from great promise into high achievement.

Satisfied that they had muzzled the police (it was later sworn to by Kurr, but never proved, that he had shortly afterwards called at Druscovitch's house and handed him two hundred sovereigns in a cigar box), Benson and Kurr took offices in Northumberland Street, Charing Cross, almost beside the back entrance of Scotland Yard where they could immediately be reached by either Meiklejohn or Druscovitch should it become necessary. There they set up business under the name of Brooks & Co. They wasted no time in putting their scheme into practice and a first issue of *Sport* was rushed out.

Sport was largely the creation of Benson and was written by him. The leader was his masterpiece and the core of the whole fraud. It referred in detail to the fact that money could be made by betting if a person was guided by expert advice, and cited the case of a Mr Andrew Montgomery. Mr Montgomery, it said, had started with nothing and yet in a comparatively short time had amassed no less than £165,000. From this great sum he had donated £1,800 to the Lancashire Distress Fund and had helped other charities similarly. With a final and typical flourish of superlative Bensonian effrontery it went on to say that Mr Montgomery had offered his services to the Jockey Club to advise on betting and on 'the reorganization of our national sport', an offer which was even then under consideration. Mr Montgomery's address was, oddly enough, that of Brooks & Co. and he was prepared to offer the services of his unrivalled

145

expertise to any of those fortunate people who received his circulars and were prepared to avail themselves of them.

Benson translated *Sport* into French under the title of *Le Sport* and five hundred copies were printed in that language to go out with the circulars which were also Benson's creation and also written in French. The paper was actually printed in Edinburgh, but to dress the whole thing up a false name and address in Paris for its printer was stamped on it.

In addition, the obliging Mr Montgomery recommended to prospective clients three bookmakers with whom they were advised to do business and to whom they should send their cheques. These were Mr Charles Jackson of St James's Place, Mr Jacob Francis of Cleveland Row and Mr Richard Gregory of Duke Street. Rooms were taken at these addresses and in these names, but of course the bookmakers did not exist at all and the addresses were mere collection-places operated by Kurr's brother Frederick and an employee called Bale. By the end of August all was ready and the circulars, accompanied by copies of *Le Sport*, went out.

The fraud succeeded beyond the conspirators' wildest dreams. The 'notaries and gentry' of the Marne and Garonne fell over each other in their anxiety to follow the obliging Mr Montgomery's betting systems and to entrust their money to his nominated bookmakers. Within a fortnight Kurr and Benson were showing a clear profit of over £15,000. Had they been satisfied at that point and then closed down the operation as they had done before, it is probable that they would have got clean away with their spoils, but they were convinced that on this occasion they had complete protection from the police and indeed Meiklejohn was frequently in and out of the office keeping himself abreast of how things were going. He was, too, constantly asking for 'his whack', complaining that he was 'short of brass' and requesting 'a pony to be going along with if it won't inconvenience you which I know it will not'. To keep him quiet they gave him money to buy a house — about £400. Meiklejohn, therefore, they knew they had completely in their power, but they were still not quite certain of Druscovitch. Questioned on this point, Meiklejohn told them: 'You can rely on him as you can on me.' Reassured and, as is the way of swindlers, always greedy for more, they pressed on. In so doing they over-reached themselves.

Among the many investors to be taken in by Mr Montgomery, the most heavily involved was a certain Madame Marie Cecil de Goncourt of the Department of the Marne. She had received the letters and circulars and a copy of *Le Sport* and had been completely convinced by them. Between 1 and 20 September she sent to the various bookmakers recommended to her by Mr Montgomery sums of money amounting to the almost unbelievable total of just on £18,000. Madame de Goncourt was a rich and gullible woman but she was not the only one. In her defence and that of the others it must be said that the articles and circulars were, as was conceded by all who saw them, quite brilliantly done. When they came into Druscovitch's hands a little later he exclaimed on reading them: 'Talk about Victor Hugo! I never read such French in my life!' And all Madame de Goncourt's brother could do when she showed them to him was to keep on repeating '*Mon Dieu! Mon Dieu!*' as he perused them.

That, however, came later. During those few weeks Madame de Goncourt was as happy as if she had stumbled on a goldmine, since in return for the money she sent she received orders for payment of 20,000, 30,000, 50,000, 25,000, 3,000 and no less than 125,000 francs respectively. These orders were accompanied by what appeared to be quite genuine bookmakers' statements showing how her winnings were made up. In all the equivalent of between £80,000 and £90,000 in English money was issued to her, purporting to represent her profit over those few weeks. Mr Montgomery was certainly operating for her on the grandest scale. The statements were, of course, like the cheques, all a sham.

Then came the awakening. On 20 September she received a letter from Mr Montgomery suggesting an investment of a further 30,000 francs. On going to her bankers to obtain the necessary draft the manager, whose curiosity had been aroused by the size of the previous drafts she had issued, questioned her and advised her to be cautious. She decided to withhold her next investment and at almost the same time the bank discovered that every one of the cheques or drafts issued in payment to her were worthless. They advised her to consult an English solicitor. She did so, and he quickly went to Scotland Yard to interview Chief Superintendent Williamson, Druscovitch's immediate superior. Realizing the importance of the case Williamson placed it in the hands of the head of the Foreign Bureau — Druscovitch.

Immediately he saw the papers Druscovitch was worried. Although he was not as yet certain that the matter concerned Brooks & Co. he had his suspicions, and he spoke to Meiklejohn about it. Meiklejohn, who was about to leave for Derby, asked him to mention the case to Kurr. Druscovitch went to Northumberland Street only to find that none of the principals was at home. He hung about the back entrance to Scotland Yard until at length Kurr and Benson appeared in Kurr's gig. Druscovitch beckoned to Kurr who crossed the street to speak to him.

'There's a big swindle come in from Paris,' Druscovitch said.

'Is it a racing affair?' Kurr asked him.

'No, I don't think so; it has something to do with spurious bills of exchange,' Druscovitch answered.

'Keep the case in your hands,' Kurr told him, and went off to consult with Benson as to what they should do.

That night they both decided the game was up and the following morning they went to Northumberland Street, packed their belongings and closed down the office. Benson with a typical flourish took the directory, totted up the totals against each name, and then, below them, wrote the word 'Finis' with the date against it.

They had in their possession about £12,000 in English notes, representing the balance of the money they had received from Madame de Goncourt. These notes presented them with a problem, since their numbers could be traced through the agents who had changed Madame de Goncourt's drafts. They sent for Druscovitch to try to find out whether he had been given the numbers of these notes. But Druscovitch was by now almost frantic with worry and all he would say was, 'I have given you the tip, and you must now look after yourselves.' Benson then had a brainwave. He remembered that Scottish banks did not check the numbers of notes they changed and he went off post-haste to Glasgow with the loot.

Kurr summoned Meiklejohn from Derby with the intention of having him put pressure on Druscovitch to assist them further, instructing him if necessary to offer Druscovitch more money. In fact Druscovitch did get the numbers of the notes the next day and also information that Benson was in Scotland for the purpose of changing them and there can be no doubt that he did drag his feet in pursuing the matter. There can be no doubt, too, that Meiklejohn was threatening him with exposure. 'Don't you think Williamson is going to be suspicious about all this?' he asked Meiklejohn.

'He's a calf. He'll never tumble to it in a thousand years,' was Meiklejohn's reply.

'I am in a difficulty, I must arrest somebody,' Druscovitch said, now desperate.

But, despite the fact that warrants against Benson and Kurr were now out, he took no steps to execute them. Either from him or from some source in Scotland Yard Meiklejohn obtained the numbers of the notes and communicated them to Kurr. Finding that the known numbers were not nearly so extensive as he had feared, Kurr wired them to Benson who changed most of the notes. When he returned to London, however, he found the hunt was really up for Druscovitch had taken fright and, having traced Benson to Shanklin, was bent on arresting someone. The faithful Meiklejohn was still ready to help provided the price was right, and Kurr saw to it that it was. Meiklejohn arranged an escape to Rotterdam to where Benson, Frederick Kurr and Bale went early in November, Benson taking yet another alias — this time that of Morton. In their hurry, however, they made the mistake of leaving behind in Benson's lodgings the French directory he had marked for the purpose of issuing his fraudulent circulars.

By then news of the frauds had become public. Reports of them were appearing not only in English but also in French newspapers, and advertisements were inserted concerning the possible criminal use of certain Scottish notes. The public were

149

warned to watch for them and report anyone attempting to change them. A reward of £1,000 was offered for information leading to the arrest of the criminals.

Benson and his friends spent freely in their hotel at Rotterdam; they also talked too much and too loudly. The owner of the hotel became suspicious and when they attempted to change a large-denomination Scottish note he communicated with the police who moved in and arrested the three men. Scotland Yard was informed and extradition proceedings started.

Kurr had remained in England under cover and using an alias. He was in constant touch with Meiklejohn who immediately informed him of what had happened. Meiklejohn was acquainted with a crooked police court solicitor called Froggatt and the three men consulted as to the best course that should now be taken. Kurr was told that the Dutch police were always reluctant to hand over persons in their custody unless they were satisfied beyond all possible doubt that their identity had been proved, and that they were notoriously difficult in their demands for such proofs. Audacious to the last, Kurr suggested sending a telegram to the governor of the prison where the others were held, stating that they were not the wanted men and instructing him to release them. Froggatt was told to draft the telegram and wrote out the following: 'Find Morton and the two men you have in custody are not those we want. Officer will not be sent over. Liberate them. Letter follows. — Carter, Scotland Yard.'

'Won't old Williamson scratch his head when he sees this,' Froggatt said as he handed it to Kurr for despatch.

It was a gambler's throw and it very nearly succeeded, for on receipt of the telegram the governor was about to act on it and free his prisoners when a subordinate suggested he would be wise to check its authenticity. In the meantime Froggatt, having told Kurr, 'A £50 note will go a long way over there,' was sent to Rotterdam with money in his pocket to try to bribe the magistrate if the telegram failed in its purpose.

None of these attempts succeeded, though Froggatt did see Benson who had by now remembered leaving the damning evidence of the directory behind him. He told Froggatt to retrieve it, which Froggatt tried to do only to find that the police had been before him.

Ultimately extradition warrants were issued against the three men. Druscovitch and four other officers were sent to bring them back. The wretched Druscovitch was by now in a terrible state. On the boat he sent the other officers out of the cabin and spoke to Benson in French, saying that he had accepted a loan of £60 from Kurr believing him to be a very different man from what he was. Benson asked him if Madame de Goncourt was in London. On being told that she was, he said that they intended to settle with her and that the whole matter might drop. Through the medium of Froggatt this was, in fact, done, and Madame de Goncourt, not being anxious to publicize her folly, agreed to waive all charges if her money was returned to her. But it was too late for any settlement. Although she proved a most reluctant witness the mass of evidence against the conspirators was overwhelming. In April 1877 Benson received a sentence of fifteen years' penal servitude and Kurr one of ten. The lesser members of the gang were sentenced to shorter terms of varying degrees of severity.

During the long trial no hint was given of police involvement. If Druscovitch was, as he thought, under some suspicion, no steps were taken then to investigate either his or Meiklejohn's activities. There was and always has been a strong suspicion that others, higher up than either Druscovitch or Meiklejohn, were implicated. When a colleague had asked Druscovitch how he was getting on with the Turf swindle he had replied feelingly: 'Damn the turf swindle, I wish I had never heard of it,' and he went on to say: 'I have documents in my hands with which I could smash two.' One of these may or may not have been the complacent and apparently ineffective Chief Superintendent Williamson, who must have been even a bigger 'calf' than Meiklejohn thought him if he did not suspect something. But in June his and his superior's hands were forced, for in that month Kurr and Benson informed on the two police officers.

The evidence produced by Benson and Kurr showed that Froggatt had also played an active part in their efforts to subvert justice. In October 1877 the three men were tried at the Old

Bailey and all were convicted. Despite the jury's strong recommendation to mercy in the case of Druscovitch, 'on account of the circumstance under which he was first induced to become acquainted with the convicts and on account of his previous good character', he received the same sentence as the others — two years with hard labour.

So ended the Great Turf Frauds with all their perpetrators safely behind bars, put there largely, except in the case of Druscovitch, by their own greed. It is impossible not to feel some sympathy for Druscovitch. Meiklejohn, who may well have been at the heart of the whole affair, which certainly would never have got off the ground without him, had his house and his share of the spoils. Kurr and Benson must have had an immense amount put away if they were able to offer Madame de Goncourt the return of her money in exchange for the hope of freedom. But Druscovitch had nothing but the ashes of a ruined career.

CHAPTER 8

Why Was Craganour Disqualified?
The 1913 Derby

WHEN IN 1910 Major Eustace Loder, of Eyrefield Lodge, The Curragh, bred a bay colt by Desmond out of Veneration II, he set in train a series of events which were to culminate in the most sensational Derby ever run — that of 1913. A cold, reserved man who was shy almost to the point of morbidity and whose friendship was given only to very few, a bachelor and a martinet, Loder reserved his affections for the two passions of his life — his regiment, the 12th Lancers, and his horses. While a serving soldier he won the Grand Military Gold Cup twice and the Conyngham Cup at Punchestown no less than four times with the best steeplechaser he owned, Covert Hack. He bred, owned and raced the peerless filly, Pretty Polly, and in 1906, the year she retired, he won the Derby with Spearmint for whom he had paid only 300 guineas as a yearling. That year, 1906, he was elected a member of the Jockey Club.

Veneration's foal apparently did not impress him and he was culled. Along with his dam, despite the fact that she was a half-sister to Pretty Polly, he was sold by Loder to the Sledmere Stud in Yorkshire for £1,700. In due course the colt was sent by the Sledmere Stud to the Doncaster Yearling Sales where he made top price and was knocked down to the bid of Mr Bower Ismay. Mr Ismay called the colt Craganour, naming him from a hill on his estate at Dalnaspidal in Perthshire.

Bower Ismay was the youngest son of T. H. Ismay who had

bought the White Star flag back in the 1860s and made a
fortune with the great liners he commissioned to sail under it in
the name of the White Star Line. His elder brother, J. Bruce
Ismay, had succeeded his father as chairman of the Line and
ran the family business. The brothers were close friends and
had married sisters, Constance and Florence Schieffelin of
New York.

Unlike his brother, Bower Ismay had sporting tastes and he
also had the means to indulge them. Steeplechasing was his first
love and his jumpers were trained for him by the famous Tom
Coulthwaite at Hednesford. Refusing the offer of a commission,
he had served as a trooper throughout the South African War.
On his return he began to develop his interests on the flat and
sent his horses to be trained by W. T. Robinson at Foxhill.
Robinson, universally known as 'Jack' Robinson, ran a betting
stable and had brought off some tremendous coups in his time.
A big, red-faced man with a choleric temper whose outbursts,
irrespective of the company he was in, had made him enemies,
Robinson was not looked upon with favour by the ruling
establishment of the time. Ismay, however, was not a betting
owner; he took pride in the fact that his horses were run openly
and to win. But he was never a great judge of either horses or
racing.

Some years before his purchase of Craganour, Ismay had
formed an attachment with Loder's sister-in-law. This developed into a long-standing affair of which Loder violently
disapproved. Whether his attitude sprang from personal dislike,
offended morality, or the unreasonable disdain then felt by the
older landed classes for those whose origins and wealth came
from trade is not known. But that it existed is undeniable for
Loder took no pains to conceal it, and felt so strongly that it has
even been said that he told a friend he would ruin Ismay
socially. This may or may not be true, but he would have
undoubtedly blocked any attempt to elect Ismay to the Jockey
Club had he shown a 'desire to explore those roads which might
lead to membership', to use the words of Sydney Galtrey, the
then Hotspur of the *Daily Telegraph* and a universally respected
racing writer who knew both men. But Ismay had no wish at all

to explore those roads; social pretensions played no part in his character or way of life.

The Ismays were a united family, proud, reserved and shy. T. H. Ismay, the founding father, had refused a baronetcy when King Edward VII offered one to him. He had also at first opposed the marriage of his favourite son, James, to Lady Margaret Seymour, the eldest daughter of the Marquis of Hertford, since he held that trade and aristocracy should not mix. Social ambitions were abhorrent both to him and his descendants. Bower Ismay therefore went his own way and kept his horses where he wanted them, unheeding of the dictates of society or the ruling few.

There can be little doubt, however, that the animosity felt for him by Loder was mutual and that something approaching a family feud existed between Loder and the Ismays. It has been suggested, probably correctly, that it was this which impelled Bower Ismay to pay top price for Loder's 'cull' in the hope that, if the colt turned out well, he would be in the position to fling Loder's misjudgment in his face and hurt him where he would feel it most — in his self-esteem as a breeder and judge of blood-stock. If this was his intention it must soon have appeared to him that he was going to be successful, for from the moment he started to work the colt Robinson formed a high opinion of him and told Ismay that he might well have a coming champion on his hands.

So matters stood early in 1912. To complete the picture it is now necessary to return to J. Bruce Ismay, the chairman of the White Star Line. Bruce Ismay had his full share of the family's shyness and reserve which in his case had been exacerbated by the stern and impersonal treatment he had received from his father when he was being schooled to succeed to the chairmanship. When he did take over he concealed his shyness and sensitivity beneath a brusque and autocratic manner. Detesting publicity, he was terse with the press and refused all requests for interviews, directing reporters instead to the Line's publicity department. None of these things made for popularity with public and press, and were no help to him in the appalling calamity which was about to befall him.

155

As chairman, Bruce Ismay had taken a personal interest in the design, building and launching of the then latest and greatest of the White Star liners, the *Titanic*. Shortly before he sailed in her on her maiden voyage he had for reasons of his own determined to resign from the chairmanship of the Line, and had done so. For reasons of company policy this was not made public at the time and it led to misunderstanding later on.

As all the world knows, the *Titanic* foundered on that maiden voyage through striking an iceberg and went down with the loss of over fifteen hundred lives. Bruce Ismay was among the survivors. As a result he suffered from a campaign of obloquy drummed up by hysterical outbursts of vilification in the American press. One paper went so far as to carry a cartoon of him sitting in a lifeboat looking at the sinking liner, the caption underneath reading: THIS IS J. BRUTE ISMAY.

That both criticism and abuse were misconceived and un-founded did little to help Ismay, who was completely cleared by the Senate hearing, for these calumnies pursued him back to Britain. In fact Ismay had assisted everyone in his area on the starboard side of the ship into the boats. As the last boat — an emergency collapsible, all the regular lifeboats having already pulled away — was being lowered he was seen by a ship's officer to be the only passenger remaining on that part of the deck. This officer ordered him to take his place in the boat. It is an absolute rule at sea that when a ship is in danger a passenger must obey the orders of a uniformed ship's officer without question or argument. Ismay did, in fact, protest and was once more informed that no others remained except himself and was again ordered to get into the boat. Then and with reluctance, he obeyed. It was conclusively proved that he took no one's place and that he was the last man to leave that area of the ship. But none of this saved him from the storm of abuse which broke about his head.

On his return voyage to England Bower Ismay and his wife journeyed to Queenstown to meet him and came down the gangway with him when the ship docked at Liverpool. He then had to face the British enquiry and further insults from counsel representing the next-of-kin and the General Workers' Union.

When the enquiry closed he went with Bower Ismay to his Perthshire estate, Dalnaspidal, to recuperate.

Although in his judgment Lord Mersey, the president of the enquiry, completely vindicated Bruce Ismay and took pains to do so in view of the conduct and allegations of counsel, the press still hounded him and public vilification still pursued him.

Through it all Bruce Ismay behaved with courage and dignity. It has been reported time and again that as a result of the criticism levelled at him he resigned his position as chairman of the White Star Line and retired to his 'estate' in the west of Ireland to live out the rest of his life as a recluse. Nothing could be further from the truth. As has already been said his resignation had been tendered and accepted before ever the *Titanic* sailed. His 'estate' in the west of Ireland — in fact a fishing lodge known as The Lodge, Costello, Co. Galway — was not purchased until after the disaster and then only used as a seasonal sporting home. He and his wife (who was *not* with him in the *Titanic* as sometimes reported) continued to live at 15 Hill Street, Mayfair. He retained his directorships in other companies in which he took an active interest, and managed the family trust with skill and success. But, although he concealed it as best he could, his spirit was shattered by the injury done to his name and reputation, from which indeed he never truly recovered.

It has been necessary to set all this down in some detail to demonstrate the extent of the animosity stirred up against Bruce Ismay and the natural bitterness and resentment felt by his brother and all his family as a result of it. It is also true that all who carried the Ismay name suffered to some degree from the public feeling against their brother.

While all these terrible events were taking place Bower Ismay's colt Craganour was triumphantly commencing his two-year-old career and appearing more and more likely to fulfil the high hopes his trainer entertained for him. In his first season's racing, from six starts he won five times, and these victories included the Champagne Stakes and the Middle Park Plate. He was ridden throughout the season by W. Saxby. Here again there is a suggestion that Ismay's choice of Saxby as his jockey had more than mere appreciation of his abilities behind it, for Saxby was only a moderate jockey at best. He was held to have been outridden and outclassed by Danny Maher when Craganour suffered his only defeat as a two-year-old — by a head in the Molecomb Stakes at Gatwick. But, more important perhaps to Ismay than his riding abilities or lack of them, he was a protégé of Loder's.

Saxby's father was a sergeant-major in the 12th Lancers during the time Loder had been that regiment's adjutant. Loder had seen the boy riding, liked his style and had arranged for him to be apprenticed to Sam Pickering at Newmarket. The boy had seen his indentures out, he frequently rode Loder's horses, and Loder considered that he had first claim on him. To have his protégé taken from him to be given rides on the colt he had culled, who had turned into the leading two-year-old of 1912 and winter favourite for the Derby, was pointed to say the least.

Loder himself had been elected a steward of the Jockey Club in 1912. The following spring, in the ordinary course of events, he would have assumed the duties of senior steward, but he had contracted Bright's disease and he asked to be relieved of them.

Early in 1913, during the jumping season, the running of one of Bower Ismay's horses caused Tom Coulthwaite to be reported to the senior stewards. At the subsequent enquiry the stewards refused to accept Coulthwaite's explanation and withdrew his licence to train. Though Ismay was in no way implicated he let it be known that he felt the sentence was both unjustified and unfair and this, coupled with what had happened over the *Titanic* disaster, must have made him feel that the whole world, and especially that part of it represented by the racing authorities, was ranged against him and his horses. But his answer to them all would come on the day Craganour won the Derby, which the colt was giving every indication of being capable of doing.

Having headed the Free Handicap of 1912 with 9st 4lb, Craganour seemed certain to justify that position in the coming season for he continued to please his trainer in his work. Robinson liked to get his horses out early and Craganour's first appearance before the Two Thousand Guineas was the Union Jack Stakes at Liverpool in the opening week of the 1913 season. Looking backward in condition, he was beaten by a colt called Flippant to whom he was giving 7lb. Little weight was given by the stable to this defeat and he went forward as favourite for the Guineas, which everyone confidently expected him to win. He started at 3—1.

Saxby was again given the ride and Major Loder was the senior acting steward at the Guineas meeting. Craganour set off in front and — or so it appeared to virtually everyone present except the judge, C. E. Robinson — won comfortably by at least a length from Mr W. Raphael's Louvois, ridden by Johnny Reiff. But when the numbers went into the frame it was seen that Mr Robinson had given the verdict to Louvois by a head. The Rowley mile was wider in those days than it is now and the two horses were racing on opposite sides of the course. Nevertheless it seemed inconceivable to most experienced racing men that Robinson could have made such a mistake. When Dawson Waugh, the trainer of Louvois, was told that his colt's number had gone up as the winner, he turned to his informant and said: 'They've made a bloomer. They'll damn soon take it down.' But they did not. The number stayed up. And, despite the outcry on the course, the stewards, headed by Loder, made no effort to interview Robinson concerning his decision. Saxby roundly declared in the hearing of all that he had won by a length and a half. Certainly he had ridden a most confident race, so much so that those few who could be found to agree with the judge's decision held that he had been over-confident, had not even bothered to shake up Craganour at the finish, and had allowed himself to be caught by Louvois' late run.

The storm broke in the press next day. Most of the criticism was directed against the judge but Saxby, too, was not spared. Robinson attempted to justify himself and to place the blame on Saxby by remarking to one journalist: 'They are saying that Saxby won on Mr Ismay's horse. What they should say is that he *ought* to have won.'

The wildest rumours flew about the racing world. The suggestion has since been made, and even then was whispered, that Loder had told Saxby to lose the race and had gone so far as to instruct the judge not to give it to Craganour in a close finish. This seems far-fetched now and was probably more so then in view of Loder's standing both socially and in racing, but personal enmities and clashes of personality can produce strange reactions in the most well-balanced of men, and Loder was suffering from a disease which can cloud the judgment and make one act irrationally. He may have been glad Craganour lost — he would scarcely have been human, given his background, had he not been — and have said so publicly and indiscreetly, but it is unlikely that he took steps to ensure his defeat.

But the rumours must have come to the ears of Ismay and Robinson. Saxby had ridden Craganour in all his previous races and given satisfaction. Something other than mere disapproval of his riding in that one race must have impelled them to act as they did. It must be remembered, too, that Ismay himself was still suffering from his family's vilification at the hands of the press and public after the sinking of the *Titanic*, he was burning with resentment at Coulthwaite's treatment by the authorities, he would be ready to believe anything of Loder, and despite his experience, he had never quite grasped the realities of racing. All these things may have provided the motives for what happened next. At all events the blame for Craganour's defeat — whether from sheer over-confidence and bad riding or for other more sinister reasons — was placed by the colt's connections squarely on Saxby's shoulders and he was stood down.

Saxby was furious and indignant as, on the face of it, he had every right to be. His riding of the colt had never been questioned before and now he was being removed from the saddle after a race virtually everyone but the judge considered he had won.

Having stood Saxby down Ismay and Robinson had to look for another jockey. Their choice fell on Danny Maher, the brilliant and charming American who was then riding for Lord Rosebery on a retainer of £5,000 a year. Craganour's next race was to be the Newmarket Stakes over ten furlongs. Lord Rosebery had no runner in the race and Maher took the ride.

Louvois was also in the race and his connections thought that the extra distance would suit him and enable him to confirm the Guineas placing with Craganour. This did not happen. Adopting much the same tactics of 'waiting in front' as Saxby in the Guineas, Maher won easily by a length and a half from Mr J. B. Joel's Sun Yat with Louvois a further two lengths away third. This result confirmed the opinion of most judges that Craganour should have won the Guineas and would win the Derby. His price for the big race shortened, but not as much as many expected, for once more rumour got to work. Suggestions were made that he was not pleasing his trainer in his final preparation and that all was not well with him. More importantly, it soon became clear that no final riding arrangements had been made for him.

Both Ismay and Robinson wanted Maher to ride the favourite and both believed that he would be released to do so. But Lord Rosebery had a filly, Prue, entered in the race. Few, including her owner, believed that she had any chance of winning, but she was not entered in the Oaks and her trainer, Fred Pratt, was anxious that she should run. The year before a filly, Tagalie, ridden by Johnny Reiff, had won the Derby for Mr Raphael, the owner of Louvois. This may have influenced Pratt in his persistence that Prue should run and may well also have influenced Ismay and Robinson in their subsequent choice of a jockey.

Lord Rosebery himself did not wish to deny Maher the chance of riding the favourite. But one of Maher's qualities which made him liked and respected throughout the racing world was his loyalty to his retaining owners and trainers. If Prue was to run, even if she had not the remotest chance, he insisted that he would stand by his retainer and ride her. He refused all the inducements and blandishments which the connections of Craganour could offer and also turned down the release from his obligations to the stable which Lord Rosebery, with a true sporting gesture, was prepared to give him. It was not, however, by any means certain that Prue would in fact run. If she did not, Maher would ride the favourite. So once more rumour and speculation proliferated until Lord Rosebery put an end to it all by writing to Galtrey, one of the leading racing correspondents of the day, as follows: 'I have tried my very best for two days to get him [Maher] to ride Craganour and let me find a jockey who would do for an outsider like Prue. But he says he insists on riding Prue. . . . That is how the matter stands, and as I am afraid will stand.' And Galtrey broke the news in the press.

Now Ismay and his trainer had to look elsewhere for a jockey. Most, but not all, of the leading English jockeys were engaged. The choice did not fall on any of those others who were free nor did they return to Saxby. Instead they went to France and approached Johnny Reiff, who accepted.

It was neither a wise nor a fortunate decision and no one knows what prompted it. Reiff was a brilliant jockey. He had already won the Derby twice, the first time on Boss Croker's Orby in 1907 and then on the filly Tagalie the year before. In addition he had won that year's Guineas on Louvois by beating Craganour in the disputed decision. But his reputation was far from good. With his elder brother, Lester, he had been brought over from America while still a boy by the American trainer, Wishard, who was himself controlled by an unscrupulous professional gambler, Drake. In those early days Reiff dressed like a schoolboy; he was petted in the paddock by racing ladies and, because of his innocent looks and mode of dress, earned the sobriquet 'Knickerbocker' Reiff. His actions belied his apparent innocence. When his elder brother Lester was warned off the English Turf he went with him to France where his undoubted abilities brought him success, but his reimportation, especially on the hottest Derby favourite for years, was popular with neither his fellow jockeys nor the authorities. Much sympathy was felt for Saxby, too, who was then given the ride on Louvois. It was openly said that the English jockeys resented the presence of Reiff on Craganour and would see that he had a rough passage. To make matters worse it was also reported that the French jockeys, of whom there were several, were in turn determined to do what they could to get their crack, Nimbus, first past the post.

All these things heightened the ill-feeling current at the time between English jockeys and their French counterparts, for it was held that English owners and trainers went too often to France for their jockeys on big occasions and in big races. This was put into words by the *Sporting Life* reporter who complained: 'J. Clark was without a mount in the Derby. Yet many owners went to France for their riding talent. There are few horsemen in any country who are more capable than Clark who acts as first jockey for Lord Durham.'

Despite everything the threats to Craganour were still held to be few. Shogun, who had been ranked second to Craganour in the Free Handicap was second favourite at 6—1. He was to be ridden by Frank Wootton, a brilliant jockey who had been a boy wonder in his time. Wootton had ridden Flippant to beat Saxby on Craganour in the Liverpool race. If he had a fault it was a fondness for the rails which occasionally lost him races he might have won, and which was to cost him dear in the coming Derby. Louvois was held in some quarters to be likely to give Saxby the opportunity of confounding his critics and confirming the Guineas result, despite the fact that he was now suspected of having two ways of running and had not been working well at home. Nimbus, the French challenger, a most handsome colt, was believed in his own country to have the beating of them all and a great throng of enthusiasts had crossed over from France to cheer him on. Amongst the outsiders Mr W. Hall Walker's Great Sport had attracted attention in the ante-post market. He was to be ridden by yet another French importation, George Stern. An Englishman who had lived all his life in France, Stern frequently came to England to ride in the big races. He neither earned nor courted popularity with stewards or public, but he was a highly competent jockey who could hold his own anywhere when it came to rough-riding.

Among those who were not even thought of by anyone was Mr A. P. Cunliffe's bay colt Aboyeur. He was by Desmond, thus having the same sire as Craganour, but that, so far, seemed his sole claim to distinction, even though Desmond had not yet sired a classic winner. Aboyeur had had six starts as a two-year-old and had won only one of them, the Champagne Stakes at the Bibury Club meeting where he beat nothing of any account. In the Free Handicap he had been given 7st 9lb, 23lb less than Craganour.

Mr Cunliffe was the leading member of what came to be known as the Druid's Lodge Confederacy. His horses were trained at Druid's Lodge, Netheravon, by J. Fallon under the supervision of Captain W. B. Purefroy. The stable was remote enough to suffer little from the attentions of touts, who were in any case summarily handled if they were caught. Here some tremendous betting coups in big handicaps were hatched early in the century. It was generally believed that Mr Cunliffe plotted these coups and Captain Purefroy carried them out. In conditions of extreme secrecy they were worked out down to the last detail, the actual placing of the bets being carried out with such skill that the most astute bookmakers failed to determine the actual weight of the money being laid and where it was coming from.

Aboyeur had one run before the Derby, finishing fourth in the Easter Stakes at Kempton. He was difficult to train, for, apart from suspect tendons, he had a savage temperament. Still Mr Cunliffe and his trainer sensed that he had ability some-where and were determined to run him. They devoted consider-able care and attention to him; his legs stayed sound and it was decided to give him a final gentle winding-up gallop the Sunday before the race.

Because of Aboyeur's unruly disposition and tendency to attack other horses on the gallops, Hughie Murphy, a tough ex-steeplechase jockey regarded as the hardiest of the lads at Druid's Lodge, had been given the task of riding him through-out his preparation. Murphy was on him in that final gallop and when they pulled up the colt was seen to be lame. Fallon immediately told Murphy to take him home and not to wait until the other horses had worked. Murphy got down to take the weight off his back before walking him to the stable. Then, as he afterwards told Frank Brown, the famous amateur rider and trainer, Fallon shouted at him: 'Don't do that, he's finished this time and he'll eat you before you get home if you try and lead him. Get on the bugger and ride him back, he's too lame to run on Wednesday, anyway.'

But that evening the leg was seen to be nothing like as bad as Fallon had thought and it was decided to let him take his chance in the Derby. Not only that, but the Confederacy determined to back him, quietly, at starting price and off the course. As a precaution against his attempting to savage other horses they decided to put blinkers on him, and he was to be the only runner in the Derby field to wear the 'rogue's badge' as it was then called.

All these events — the controversial result of the Guineas, the criticism of the judge, who was also due to officiate at the Derby, the known — and unfair — public vilification of the Ismays, the bad feeling between English and French jockeys, together with the wheeling and dealing over who was to ride the favourite, heightened both tension and expectation as Derby Day approached. And, unknown to anyone, something completely alien to racing was being hatched behind the scenes which would ensure that on that day, Wednesday 4 June 1913, sensation would be piled on sensation.

Emily Wilding Davidson was among the more militant — if indeed she was not the most militant — of all the WSPU or suffragettes as they were more generally known. Her militancy and the violence she advocated to attain their ends went far beyond the bounds of what many of her colleagues thought permissible, but her gaiety, personal charm and vivacity enabled her to overcome most of their criticisms. In December 1911 she had embarked on a course of arson and physical assault entirely on her own account and without the authority or permission of her leaders. She lashed a totally innocent Baptist minister from Aberdeen with a dog-whip on Aberdeen Station, explaining afterwards that she had mistaken him for Lloyd George! She went on to carry out what one of the historians of the movement described as 'solitary acts of defiance'. The most startling of these was setting fire to pillar boxes at Westminster by dropping into them lighted rags soaked in paraffin. For this she was apprehended and sentenced to six months in Holloway gaol. She proved a most intransigent prisoner. During one argument with her warders she threw herself over the railings outside her cell, falling on to the netting fixed some distance below to thwart suicide attempts. Climbing from this, she then threw herself down the iron staircase and suffered severe injuries, from which, it is said, she never wholly recovered.

The night before the Derby her room-mate observed her sewing the colours of the movement inside her coat. When asked what she was going to do, Emily Davidson replied: 'Look in the paper and you will see. I'm going to the Derby tomorrow.' Early next morning she went to suffragette headquarters and took from them two flags in their colours. One of these she wrapped around her underneath her coat. The other, furled, she carried. Thus equipped, she made her way to Tattenham Corner.

The stewards of the Epsom meeting that Wednesday were the Earl of Rosebery, Lord Wolverton and Major Eustace Loder. The last two were also stewards of the Jockey Club.

Before the race was run Robinson, a highly strung man, had been in a state of deep anxiety. Possibly because of the Ismay connection he had received an avalanche of anonymous warnings, threatening letters and prophecies of doom. When he was interviewed about Craganour's chances, he replied, as if gripped by some premonition: 'He can scarcely fail save by some stroke of bad luck, impossible to foresee.' And Saxby's father told his family and friends that Craganour would win the Derby but that he would not keep it. Where he obtained this strange piece of clairvoyance from no one knew, but he said it and went on saying it.

Derby Day itself dawned overcast and cloudy but by the time the runners paraded the sun had broken through. In the paddock Craganour stood out. In colour he was an unusually light bay and some pundits held him to be a shade on the small side. Nevertheless he looked what he was — a high-class thoroughbred, trained to the minute, ready to run for his life and a worthy Derby favourite. Others to attract attention were Day Comet and Great Sport, while Shogun was seen to be sweating up. No one took much notice of Aboyeur who was among the 100—1 others. So little did the confederacy really fancy him that no jockey had been engaged to ride him until after that last gallop. Edwin Piper usually rode as first jockey for George Edwardes, the theatrical magnate who owned the

Gaiety Theatre. Edwardes had no runner in the Derby and Piper had been asked to ride Boss Croker's Knight's Key. When Knight's Key was taken out on the Monday before the race Fallon booked Piper for Aboyeur. A West Countryman, Piper had started his career in the show ring and was far from being one of the leading jockeys. Despite this and their lack of real confidence in their runner on the morning of the race the Confederacy backed him quietly off the course at starting price. One leading S.P. office in the city stood to lose £40,000 over him, and similar bets were placed elsewhere. It must be remembered, however, that with the price at 100—1 the amounts actually laid were insignificant in the context of the Confederacy's accustomed investments on a fancied horse.

Willoughby, the starter, had them quickly away and Aboyeur almost immediately went into the lead, a position he still held when the field rounded Tattenham Corner. It seemed to many that the outsider was going to come home alone when, to a great roar of cheering, Craganour closed on him. Immediately behind were Shogun, whom Wootton had brought over to his usual position on the rails, Day Comet and Louvois.

At this point Reiff hit Craganour with his right hand. The favourite veered towards Aboyeur who promptly attempted to savage him. Reiff, to use his own words, 'Put him back,' (Donoghue, who rode in the race and saw it all, says in his reminiscences that he would have done exactly the same in his place and that Reiff was right when he said he was perfectly entitled to do this). Aboyeur then swung towards the rails, hampering Shogun and for the moment effectively boxing him in. Wootton still clung to the rails, refusing to leave them and make his run on the outside. Aboyeur then veered outwards again and once more hung on to Craganour. By now Louvois and Day Comet had come through the gap between Aboyeur and Shogun and Wootton could not have got out had he wanted to. Stern on Great Sport was also trying to get through and not caring very much about how he did it.

A general dog-fight then developed all the way to the post but there can be no doubt, and the photograph shows it, that Aboyeur was leaning on Craganour all the way. Reiff, it is true,

167

was not the man to take this sort of treatment lying down and no doubt he gave as good as he got. A few yards from the post he hit Craganour again once, hard. Craganour responded. They passed the post locked together but Craganour had his head in front. That was the distance by which the judge gave Craganour the race — a head. And that was how the numbers went up, with Louvois third and Great Sport fourth.

No one could deny that it had been a very rough race. One of the French jockeys, returning to scale, remarked that he might as well have been in a bullfight. There were, therefore, anxious faces as Craganour was led into the winner's enclosure. Cunliffe and Piper were seen in earnest conversation and immediately speculation flew about that an objection would be lodged by them. But Piper told his owner that he thought he might be in serious trouble for not keeping a straight course, which indeed he had not, being all over the track from the moment Craganour came upsides with him. It has to be remembered, too, that Mr Cunliffe was one of the few who knew of his colt's savage temperament and he may not have been anxious to publicize this. In any event, what he heard from Piper appears to have clinched his own opinion. Despite the loss of his wagers — and the Confederacy were never anxious to lose money — he let it be known that he did not intend to object.

Nevertheless there was a delay in declaring the winner all right. Robinson, who before the race had been keyed up almost to the point of breakdown, was standing beside Sydney Galtrey, perspiring in the heat and expressing in pungent language his fears of what might happen. Then, at length, the 'all right' was called. 'Thank goodness for that,' Robinson said to Galtrey. 'I was beginning to get worried.'

He spoke too soon. At almost the same instant a figure appeared at the entrance to the winner's enclosure. It was none other than Lord Durham, 'Determined Jack' as he had come to be called, the then dictator of the Turf. Although that year he was enjoying one of the few periods when he was not in the seat of power as senior steward, this did not prevent him from exercising his authority. Galtrey remembered him 'looking rather fierce and terribly serious'. 'Who', he thundered, 'has given authority for the all right to be given? Bring that horse back.' (No satisfactory explanation, incidentally, has ever been given as to why the all right was called or who called it and on whose authority. The stewards preserved complete silence on this point.)

It would almost be true to say that pandemonium followed Lord Durham's pronouncement. No one knew or could tell what was happening or had happened, for, as has been said, Cunliffe had made it quite clear that he was not going to object. There was of course no public address system in those days, but gradually the news spread that the stewards themselves had objected to the winner. Bower Ismay received the information without change of countenance, but he must have known that with Loder in the chair the dice were loaded against him.

While all this was going on another equally sensational event had taken place down the course. In the excitement of the finish very few had noticed that the King's horse, Anmer, was missing, and fewer still were aware a few minutes later of a stretcher being brought in and put down in the weighing-room. On the stretcher was the unconscious form of Herbert Jones, the royal jockey.

Emily Davidson had indeed made the headlines as she had promised she would. Somehow evading the attentions of the police on the spot, she had managed to slip under the rails just before Tattenham Corner and rush on to the course as the field thundered past. It is most unlikely that she deliberately chose the royal horse with which to interfere, since at that distance and at the pace the horses were going she could scarcely have selected the colours. But had she wanted to do so for publicity purposes she could not have made a better choice. Waving the flag in front of her, she appeared to throw herself in front of Anmer which was brought down. The colt turned a complete somersault and rolled on Jones who was knocked unconscious and badly cut about the face. There was no proper ambulance room at Epsom then, a fact which later caused considerable criticism, and Jones had to lie in the weighing-room and subsequently the jockeys' room before a temporary ambulance tent was rigged up for him. Some time later he was removed to hospital where his injuries were found to be not as serious as they had seemed and he made a rapid and complete recovery.

Miss Davidson was not so fortunate. The first diagnosis reported her as suffering from concussion, but it was later discovered that her brain had been injured. Despite an operation carried out by a leading brain surgeon sympathetic to the movement, she died on the following Sunday. The suffragettes made her a martyr and gave her a funeral accompanied by such ceremony and pomp as to rival, in the words of one historian, 'the obsequies of princes'. It was later revealed that shortly before the Derby a champion at Cruft's had been poisoned. The suffragettes had admitted liability, and an anonymous letter had been sent to the owner stating that for the sake of the cause they proposed to sacrifice all prize-winning animals including 'the favourite for the Derby'. It was thought that Miss Davidson might have been the author of this letter or inspired by it.

Meanwhile the stewards had convened their own objection. It was an act entirely without precedent in the Derby and they had only recently been given the powers to do so. It is important to note, too, that it was not, as it would be in modern times, a 'stewards' enquiry' into what happened during the race. It was an objection by the stewards to the winner. Thus, at a stroke, they made themselves less than impartial, for by the act of objecting themselves to the horse which had won they became prosecutors in the first instance and judges only in the second. Even without the extraordinary circumstances and complications surrounding this race, the course they took made it highly unlikely that in their secondary capacity as judges they would dismiss their own objection.

It was Loder, as he later confirmed, who was the instigator of the stewards' actions and who insisted on their making the objection. Rosebery, who had a runner, Prue, in the race, refused to sit on it, but he did not nominate anyone to act in his place and remained in the room during the entire hearing. As a result the proceedings were conducted by two stewards only. Two did not constitute a quorum, so that the whole enquiry was bad from the outset, but apparently no one, least of all Loder, took any notice of this. Wolverton was a nonentity and the enquiry was conducted to all intents and purposes by Loder alone.

The stewards' objection to the winner, presumably drafted by Loder, was on the grounds that he 'jostled the second horse'. The witnesses called were C. E. Robinson, the judge, the riders of the first and second, Reiff and Piper, together with those of the placed horses, Saxby and Stern, and, for reasons best known to themselves, Frank Wootton, who on Shogun had finished out of the money.

It is notable that Donoghue, who, although officially placed eighth, was close up behind Louvois and in a position to see the whole thing and who would have given evidence in favour of Reiff, was not called. Robinson may well have been still smarting under the criticism of having misjudged the Guineas against Craganour, and it can at least be said that he would not be prejudiced in his favour. The accuracy of Robinson's evidence which 'supported the case for the prosecution' can in any event be gauged by the fact that he did not place Day Comet at all, although it was the opinion of almost everyone else concerned (except the stewards who were too busy with other things) that Day Comet had finished third. But he was racing underneath Robinson on the rails and it seems he overlooked him completely. Edward Moorhouse, another of the great sporting writers of the day, who was by no means prejudiced in favour of Craganour, stated categorically that he knew the stewards placed much weight on Robinson's evidence, but he went on to interpret a photograph of the finish which was in his possession as clearly indicating Day Comet in third position. 'Never surely', he wrote, 'has there been greater confusion over the result of a race, and it would certainly appear that Day Comet received far less recognition than was his due.'

Saxby was a man with a grievance, and according to one reporter who spoke to the jockeys afterwards: 'Saxby, who rode Louvois, gave very damning evidence against Reiff alleging that he interfered with almost everything in the race including Louvois and Shogun.' Since in the opinion of another good judge who watched the race closely Louvois was about the only horse in it who enjoyed a comparatively clear run, this evidence should not have gone unchallenged. But Saxby was Loder's protégé and he was likely to give weight to it even without his known bias against Ismay. Wootton had already been criticized by Louis de Rothschild, the owner of Shogun, for allowing himself to be shut in and thereby perhaps losing the race. Still smarting from this rebuke, he was unlikely to give evidence uncoloured by personal feelings and he, too, blamed Reiff. 'Did Wootton blame Reiff on Craganour for the pocketing?' Sydney Galtrey asks, and goes on to comment: 'If so the stewards would get the evidence they were seeking.' Galtrey, who throughout his account gives the impression that he would like to say more than he actually did (he was writing when some of the actors in the drama were still alive), uses the word 'seeking', which must imply that the stewards — or Loder alone as it turned out — were searching for evidence on which they could justify a disqualification of Craganour.

It is an indication, too, of the manner hostile to Craganour in which Loder conducted the enquiry, that when Jack Jarvis, the trainer, met George Stern in the passage outside the stewards' room after he had given his evidence, Stern said to him: 'They're going to disqualify that bloody horse.'

The ring were freely offering 4 or 5—1 against Aboyeur being given the race, and bookmakers, because they have to be, are no bad judges of running. A few, however, including Jarvis, had come to the conclusion that Craganour would lose it and backed Aboyeur accordingly.

One might have expected that in view of the importance of the matter and the numbers of the witnesses to be examined that the stewards would give it weighty and lengthy consideration. They did not. It took them precisely fifteen minutes to conduct the enquiry and arrive at their decision, which strongly hints at some degree of prejudgement. They disqualified Craganour, placed him last, and awarded the race to Aboyeur.

When the verdict was announced Saxby, in front of the weighing-room and in sight of everyone, waved his hat in the air. He was one of the very few to agree with it and he had his own reasons for doing so. To all who saw it his action gave a clear indication of the bias his evidence must have contained.

172

It is, however, only fair to add that Jack Jarvis writes in his memoirs: 'From what I had seen with my own eyes I was sure that Craganour would lose the race.' But Jarvis at that time was only twenty-six and the opinion of Richard Marsh, trainer to King Edward VII and a far more experienced racing man than Jarvis, may be set in the balance against him: 'I shall always maintain', he wrote, 'that it was a tragic decision which was not merited.' And that indeed was how the greatest number of people, especially those who knew the background, saw it. Nor were press and public slow to point out that, although Craganour had been disqualified, no punishment had been handed out to Reiff, his rider, who, if the stewards' decision was correct, must surely have been guilty of careless riding at best and probably much more. To make matters worse, the communiqué the stewards issued did nothing to clarify matters. Indeed it only compounded the confusion.

> The stewards objected to the winner on the grounds that he jostled the second horse. After hearing the evidence of the judge and several of the jockeys riding in the race, they found that Craganour, the winner, did not keep a straight course, and interfered with Shogun, Day Comet and Aboyeur. Having bumped and bored the second horse they disqualified Craganour and awarded the race to Aboyeur.

Again this statement was much criticised. Some interpreted it as meaning that Craganour had not kept a straight course throughout the race, which was inaccurate as to fact and not in conformity with the original objection laid. Others stated that the stewards had added additional indictments to their original one, for instance not keeping a straight course, interfering with other horses as well as the second, and bumping and boring.

The statement is, of course, very badly worded but in justice to the stewards it must be said that it does, when read as a whole, give effect to their original complaint. 'Bumping and boring' the second horse is much the same as 'jostling' (an archaic word which is still in use) and it was for this that they disqualified Craganour.

Bower Ismay, like his brother the year before during the aftermath of the *Titanic* sinking, behaved with the utmost dignity throughout the whole affair. He stood alone and un-smiling as he heard the verdict which robbed him of racing's greatest prize and accepted the many commiserations he received impassively and without complaint. His attitude, Galtrey records, was that of a cynic, for which in view of the many buffetings of fate which he had received over the past eighteen months and the fact that his sworn opponent, Loder, was senior steward of the day, he had every justification. Always a thought-ful man, he behaved with the greatest generosity to Robinson and the stable lads, giving them the same presents they would have received if Craganour had been confirmed as the winner.

Robinson, however, more mercurial in temperament, was cast into the deepest misery and gloom and raged against what he considered to be the flagrant injustice of it all. The next day the reports in the sporting press, almost all of which were unanimous in condemning the decision, did little to calm things down. And, by an extraordinary coincidence, Saxby's father, who had foreseen the result and prophesied it, was found dead of a heart attack, the papers carrying the result of the race strewn around him.

Whether the fact that only two stewards had sat on the objection reached Ismay's ears cannot now be ascertained, but it looks as if it must have done, for at a late hour he reversed his original attitude of abiding stoically by the decision and decided to appeal, the grounds of the appeal being that 'the formalities had not been complied with', which of course they had not. Unfortunately for him he was too late. More than forty-eight hours, the time given in the rules for lodging such an appeal, had elapsed and the Jockey Club refused to hear it. Ismay then applied through the courts for an injunction to restrain Weatherby's paying out the prize money. The judge hearing the matter evidently considered that he had at least a stateable case for he granted Ismay an interim injunction and interim injunctions are not lightly given in matters of this sort. Then, it seems, repugnance over the whole affair and the way he had been treated overcame Ismay and dissuaded him from proceed-

174

ing further. An agent acting for Señor Martinez de Hoy of the Argentine offered him £30,000 for Craganour and he accepted. The colt never ran again, but he proved a tremendous success as a sire, getting many important winners in his new country.

Aboyeur had two other runs after the Derby and was beaten in both. It is an interesting reflection on the merits placed on the two colts by the bloodstock market that he was then sold to the Imperial Racing Club of St Petersburg for £13,000 — £17,000 less than Craganour had made. His subsequent history is obscure and he is presumed to have been lost in the Russian Revolution.

And the principal human actors? Loder, already a sick man, suffered as the Ismay family had suffered the year before from the criticism and obloquy heaped upon him by press and public for his decision. 'I have always understood', Galtrey wrote, with pardonable understatement, 'that he felt a very considerable reaction.' Certainly his obituarist in the *Bloodstock Breeders' Review*, who knew him personally, recorded that the whole affair 'caused him considerable distress of mind', as indeed it should have done, and it is probably kinder to pass no further comment on his conduct. The disqualification and its consequences may well have been responsible for the final onslaught of his illness, for he died just over a year later on 27 July 1914.

Robinson never recovered from the anguish and shock of it all. He lived for another five years, and in fact won the St Leger that same year, 1913, with Night Hawk. But his spirit was broken, his fortunes declined and he was a sick man when he died in 1918 at the age of fifty.

When World War I broke out Ismay — can this be pure coincidence? — applied for and received a commission in the 12th Lancers, Loder's former and beloved regiment. He survived the war, having served with distinction, part of the time on detachment in East Africa. Contrary to what has often been said, he did not go out of racing after Craganour's disqualification, but kept horses in training during the war and after it. In 1924 he collapsed on Euston Station and was taken to the Royal Free Hospital where he died of sleeping sickness, which he had contracted when shooting big game in Africa.

175

The Derby of 1913 was a race of tragedies. In summing up it seems clear that a grave injustice was done to an innocent man and a potentially great horse, whose services as a sire were thus lost forever to British bloodstock.

CHAPTER 9

Coat of Mail and Silver Badge

WHAT IS YOUR IDEA of a good thing in racing, Mr Barrie?'
'A useful three-year-old in a moderate two-year-old race.'
Such was, or is said to have been, the question put by the
presiding magistrate and the answer given by Peter Christian
Barrie in the police court proceedings which led to him and
several others being committed for trial at the Old Bailey as a
result of a series of particularly daring and successful Turf frauds.

The naked effrontery of the answer was typical of the man.
The offences of which he was accused took place in the winter of
1919 and the spring of 1920, when Barrie was thirty-three. He
had had a varied career. His parents had emigrated to Australia
when he was a child and he had grown up there. It was there,
too, that he had learnt to ride and manage horses, and had
ridden races as an amateur jockey. In 1915 he had joined up as a
trooper in the Australian Light Horse. At Gallipoli he was badly
wounded in the right arm. After spending six months in hospital
he was discharged as unfit for further service and was also
diagnosed to be suffering from valvular disease of the heart.
During the next two years he drove an army lorry in Wales and
then drifted into motor-car dealing. But all the time his interests
lay with horses and racing. Soon he abandoned cars for horses,
and from dealing in them began to acquire them. Those which
he kept he ran in his own or his wife's name and in some
instances he rode them himself.

177

Barrie had considerable charm; he spent freely and gave the appearance of being a man of means. By 1919 he was to all appearances prospering; he had eight horses in training in his wife's name with Horace Berg at Epsom. He was turned out by one of the best tailors in London, and he and his wife occupied a suite at the Queen's Hotel in Leicester Square.

All this was a façade. In fact he lived largely by his wits and on the fringe of the Turf underworld. He had a criminal record himself — in March 1917 he had been sentenced at Liverpool police court to two months' hard labour for stealing a cheque book and wallet from a man whose bedroom in a hotel he had been sharing. In the autumn of 1919 he was desperately hard up. Shortly before he hatched the plot for substituting a good three-year-old called Jazz for a bad two-year-old called Coat of Mail in the Faceby Plate at Stockton on 26 October he had been charged at Marylebone Police Court with obtaining £275 by means of a worthless cheque, and he had been lucky to be acquitted.

The scheme which sprang from his fertile mind was ingenious and all but reckless in its daring and audacity. One of the weaknesses in any plan for substituting a horse, or 'running a ringer' in racing parlance, is that the mastermind must have accomplices and that those accomplices must keep their mouths shut. The choice of those ready to assist in what is a serious criminal offence is obviously limited, but Barrie's acquaintance-ship with the seamier side of racing and its inhabitants was wide and varied. He decided to enlist as his first lieutenant a blood-stock dealer called Walter Hopkins with whom he was on friendly terms and whose record on the Turf was far from unblemished.

Hopkins had served his time as an apprentice, and when he became too heavy to ride, had been granted a trainer's licence. In 1909 he had been warned off after an incident in the Channel Islands. Later he applied for reinstatement and was given it, but in 1912 was again warned off for two years over the running of one of the horses in his care. The judge's comment at the hearing of the charges concerning Coat of Mail and others, that Hopkins had no proper sense of right or wrong when dealing with horses, was borne out beyond question by his actions in collaboration with Barrie beginning in September 1919.

At the time Hopkins had in his stable a completely useless two-year-old called Coat of Mail. This horse had been bred by General Baird, a member of the Jockey Club on whose behalf Felix Leach had sold it to Dawson Waugh, the Newmarket trainer, for 55 guineas in early 1919. In June Waugh passed it on to Hopkins for 90 guineas, with the stipulation that it was not to be run in England. Coat of Mail was a sickly and ill-favoured animal. From the moment it came to him Hopkins was treating it to try to bring it back to some sort of health and condition. For that reason alone it was unlikely to run in England or anywhere else for some time to come.

During the summer months William Collis, a jockey then riding in India, arrived in England with a commission to buy horses to race there for a wealthy Bombay merchant. He had known Hopkins before he left England and he sought him out in his quest for suitable stock to take to India. Hopkins introduced him to Barrie and the three became friendly.

Collis was due to return to India in October with the horses he had purchased. It seems clear that Barrie and Hopkins between them decided to use Collis as a catspaw and a means of making their substituted horse disappear by shipping him out of the country immediately after the race, for by now they had found a horse they thought well suited to be the 'ringer' in their scheme. This was Jazz, a three-year-old owned by Sir Hedworth Meux and trained by Atty Persse at Stockbridge.

Early in October Hopkins asked Persse if Sir Hedworth would sell Jazz, telling him that he wanted him for export to India. A deal was concluded on 22 October at Newbury Races by which Hopkins got Jazz for £800 again with a stipulation that the horse was not to run in England. Hopkins got £25 commission on the deal from Sir Hedworth.

Shortly afterwards Barrie, Hopkins and Collis met at the Queen's Hotel, allegedly to make arrangements for shipping to India the horses which Collis had bought. At this point it should be emphasised, and the jury later so found, that Collis was then completely in ignorance of the contemplated switch of horses at

Stockton which had been plotted by Barrie and Hopkins. Barrie in fact, giving the assumed name of 'A. Pearson' and a fictitious address in Leicester Square, had already entered Coat of Mail for the Faceby Plate and the entry had been accepted by Weatherby's.

The horses which Collis was to take to India were being assembled at Leatherhead where he had rented some stables. Jazz, however, which should have been among them, was not sent there. Instead a message was received by Persse asking him to send Jazz to Waterloo. Barrie, in the company of Walter Easton, a horse porter employed by Aldridge's, the shippers, met Jazz at Waterloo where Barrie instructed Easton to take him to King's Cross and consign him to Stockton. Easton asked Barrie the horse's name and was told it was Coat of Mail. 'Has it any chance?' Easton said. 'It has a little bit of a chance and I'm putting something on,' was Barrie's reply.

The bare-faced effrontery of the scheme now about to be played out is heightened by the fact that Jazz in no way resembled the real Coat of Mail. Coat of Mail was an ill-made, washy bay while Jazz was a brown colt of some quality. When pictures of the two horses were handed to the judge at the trial his comment that they resembled a 'before and after' advertisement was apt indeed.

Barrie, however, knew what he was about, for the Stockton racecard at that time gave no details of the colour or breeding of the horses entered. Luck played its part, too, in assisting the conspirators, for it was bitterly cold and snow was falling on and off during the afternoon which gave Barrie every excuse for keeping the horse in his box until the last minute. In addition he only brought Jazz on to the course half an hour before the off and then the horse was so fully rugged up that had anyone wished to examine him through the flurries of snow he would scarcely have been able to do so.

The betting on Coat of Mail, as might have been expected on an unknown two-year-old who had never run before, opened at 20—1. Such, however, was the weight of money poured on to him by Barrie that the price steadily shortened until at starting he was returned favourite at 5—2 in a field of eight. It has never been precisely ascertained how much Barrie cleared on this coup but his share of the course betting alone is said to have been at least £3,000. Hopkins had taken the precaution of absenting himself from the meeting and was in Brussels on the day of the race.

Having brought the horse to the course Barrie next had to find a jockey, for to make security doubly sure no jockey had been engaged prior to racing. It happened that one of the leading jockeys of the day, Walter Griggs, was without a mount in the Faceby Plate since the colt he had been engaged to ride had been found lame. Hearing this, Barrie approached him and, introducing himself in the name of Pearson, asked him to ride Coat of Mail. At first Griggs refused. Barrie, however, was persuasive and he pressed him saying that the horse had a good chance. Griggs cannot have been unaware of how Coat of Mail was shortening in the betting and in the end he consented to take the ride. By this time it was late and Griggs was brought straight to the horse's box. There was no time to take him into the ring but Griggs was not worried about this, accepting Barrie's explanation that he did not want to expose Coat of Mail to the foul weather. Mounting him outside the box, Griggs cantered straight down to the start. Drawn number one, Jazz jumped off in front, was never headed and won in a trot.

Collis had, in all innocence, travelled up with Barrie. He assisted with the betting and had had a bet himself. When he had collected and was paying Barrie, who seemed, not unnaturally perhaps, to be in a mood of euphoria, Barrie asked him if he would care to see the winning horse. At the box he turned to Collis and said: 'Well now, do you recognize him?' When Collis said that he did not, Barrie said: 'That is your horse, Jazz. I have run him.'

Collis was furious. He accused Barrie of being a swindler, said there would be a terrible row about it and that it was he who would get into trouble, not Barrie.

'Don't worry. It is quite all right. It's easy to ring horses over here. I'll see you get your share,' Barrie told him.

'How much?' Collis asked him. It was those two words which

181

were to implicate him in the fraud and with which he fell into Barrie's cleverly baited trap.

'I've backed the horse heavily in London,' Barrie said. 'If you keep your mouth shut I'll see you get £1,000.'

Collis swallowed the bait and agreed to keep quiet, but he returned to London a badly frightened man. As a result of what had happened he did not ship Jazz to India nor did he return himself, but hung around London endeavouring, unsuccessfully, to collect the £1,000 from Barrie.

The bookmakers might have been swindled and the authorities fooled that day at Stockton but the racing press were not. Next morning the race made headlines. 'The Stockton Coup comes off' ran one. 'Easy victory for Coat of Mail' was another. More significantly, perhaps, a further comment was given prominence: 'Coat of Mail's connections were not entertaining an angel unawares.'

Barrie, however, proceeded on his own imperturbable way. Back in London, in the name of 'A. Pearson' he collected his winning stake from Weatherby's. It amounted to £167 19s 6d. He cashed the cheque at Nicholl's in Regent Street, bought his wife a fur coat for £27 10s and pocketed the change. Out of this he sent Hopkins £90 as his share of the stake. This is the only money from his winnings that he appears to have given to either Hopkins or Collis at any time.

Alerted by the press comment, Weatherby's decided to ask 'Mr Pearson' for further information about himself and Coat of Mail. They wrote three times requesting the name of his trainer. It is not at all clear how these letters reached Barrie, since the address he had given when making the entry was a purely fictitious one. Presumably they must have done so in the same way as the cheque for the stakes. At all events it is clear that he did receive them and to the last he despatched the following reply:

Coat of Mail has been at my farm for some two months, and has been not exactly in training but out at exercise with hunting horses under the charge of my groom. About a fortnight previous to his running at Stockton I asked several trainers to take him but unfortunately they had no boxes vacant. . . . I am sorry if I have transgressed any of your rules, but I was led to understand that a horse trained by the owner on his private grounds could be classed as training privately.

This letter, as counsel was to comment at the hearing, was a highly ingenious one. It pleaded penitence but carefully gave no information at all.

Collis, meanwhile, unable to obtain his money from Barrie with whom he had a stand-up row in a hotel bar, calling him a common swindler at the top of his voice before walking out, was unable to keep his mouth shut. He met a friend from India, Victor Bowley, also a jockey, and poured out the whole story to him. Bowley gave him cold comfort, saying he knew Barrie and that Collis had been a fool to have had anything to do with him.

More importantly, Hopkins ran into Collis unexpectedly in London. 'Hello,' he said to him. 'I thought you were half-way to India by now.' Collis once more gave chapter and verse for all that had happened at Stockton, complaining that he could not get his share of the take from Barrie, and told Hopkins that he still had Jazz who was costing him good money to keep. He then asked Hopkins if he would take Jazz off his hands. Perhaps realizing the danger Collis's loose tongue threatened, Hopkins agreed, saying that he would try to get permission from Sir Hedworth Meux and Atty Persse to run him over hurdles. He succeeded in this, ran Jazz at Cardiff and won. Collis was not told that Jazz was either entered or off. He did not have a bet nor did he see any of the stake money. His resentment increased and, foolishly for himself, he continued to talk.

Very soon, as one of the witnesses said at the trial, it was common knowledge all over the West End of London that Barrie had run a ringer at Stockton and had cleaned up. At last the authorities decided to move and called in Scotland Yard. Undeterred, however, Barrie was planning another and even more audacious coup.

On 6 September he had bought a useful bay mare called Shining More for 540 guineas, put her in his wife's name and

sent her to Horace Berg to be trained. She won a hurdle at
Cheltenham on 10 November. On 21 November she was second
in a field of ten at Cardiff, and two days later ran second again at
Folkestone. Barrie planned to run her next in the Malvern
Selling Hurdle at Cheltenham on 29 December. It is hardly
necessary to add that he did not intend to run her under her own
name nor as owned or entered by himself or his wife.

The race was a selling race and so it was essential, in order to
complete and cover up the contemplated fraud, that she should
be bought in if she won. Since it was also essential for Barrie's
purposes that his own name should be kept out of the proceedings, he had to get someone else to bid for her and make sure
of buying her in. So there had to be an accomplice, and on this
occasion it was best that he should be a mug where racing was
concerned. Barrie looked around and in no time at all he found
not one mug but two.

Cyril Sharwood Lawley ran a garage at Hampstead known as
the Silver Badge Motor Works. He had got to know Barrie when
he was dealing in cars and they had remained on friendly terms
on and off ever since. In December 1919, when Barrie came to
Lawley and asked him if he would enter a mare at Cheltenham
for him, using Lawley's name as the owner, he at first demurred
and asked Barrie why he wanted this done. Barrie, ever ready
with a convincing tale, told him that he had bought the mare
cheap at a sale of Army remounts, and that when he put her in
training and worked her he had found she was something
special and sure to win races. He himself was a well-known
owner; if he entered the mare in his own name, he said, the odds
would be so short it would not be worthwhile backing her,
adding that at the moment he needed a touch as he was a bit
short of cash. As a further inducement he said that, if the mare
won, Lawley was welcome to the stake. If the mare did not win,
Barrie said, then Lawley would have had a good day out and he
would see that he was not a loser over it.

Lawley, who was himself low in funds, swallowed this whole
or said he did. He also said that he had raced a little in Rhodesia
before the war and that this sort of thing was quite a common
occurrence there. The two of them then sat down to compose a

184

letter to Weatherby's. The official who received it thought it seemed 'quite innocent and straightforward'. Written on headed paper reading 'Silver Badge Motor Works', it stated that Lawley had purchased a bay mare at a sale of Army remounts at Bristol, asked that it should be entered in the Malvern Selling Hurdle at Cheltenham, and requested permission to name it 'Silver Badge'. To add an extra touch of verisimilitude the letter was signed 'Cyril S. Lawley, Lieut RE', which rank he had, in fact, held during the war. There had been no sale of remounts at Bristol or anywhere else on the date given, nor had Barrie ever bought any animal at such a sale. The entry was accepted and there, for the moment, Lawley's part in the conspiracy rested.

The other mug was a very different individual indeed. Norman Weisz was a pearl merchant in Hatton Garden, a rich bachelor with a taste for gambling and an unblemished business reputation. Weisz had been born in Hungary in 1879 in comparatively humble circumstances. Apprenticed to a jeweller, after serving his time he had come to England at the age of eighteen. By hard work and diligence he had been able to set up on his own account and had prospered. In 1914 he had become a naturalized British subject and by 1919 he was enjoying an income of £10,000 a year.

At some time in that year he had grown bored with business life and had decided that an interest in the Turf would add spice to it. Knowing nothing of racing or horses, he first plunged enthusiastically into betting. Soon, however, he was the proud owner of a horse called Winkle which he ran in the *nom de course* of 'Mr Norman', a practice then permitted. Winkle ran frequently, he backed it each time it ran, but it never won. When he went racing he frequented tipsters and touts, giving as much as £25 for a tip if he felt it was a winning one. He had accounts with numerous bookmakers and betted heavily both on and off the course and his accounts almost always showed a loss. One of his principal bookmakers later described how, as an act of compassion, he had once suggested a winning wager to Weisz. When the horse did indeed win and Weisz came to collect he was so pleased with the tip that he presented the bookmaker

185

with a pearl pin! At the trial a friend of his described him in answer to counsel as 'an absolute ass on a racecourse' — a characterization that could not have been bettered.

In the autumn of 1919 an unnamed trainer introduced Weisz to a Mr Gilbert Marsh, describing Marsh as 'a millionaire metal merchant in the city'. Marsh was nothing of the sort; he was in fact a confidence man. He told Weisz he could introduce him to an Indian maharajah who wanted to buy 'thousands of pounds' worth' of jewels, and then tried to persuade Weisz to buy a half share in a useless two-year-old called Bruce Lodge which Marsh assured him would win the Derby next year. Showing some sense for once, Weisz refused this offer.

Marsh and Barrie were acquainted and Marsh was in some way connected with the Coat of Mail coup, for he had telephoned Weisz on the day of the race to back Coat of Mail for him, which Weisz did. Shortly after the race Weisz was introduced to Barrie and told him about the Coat of Mail bet, at which Barrie warned him to beware of Marsh. Later that month Marsh inveigled Weisz into a card game at his flat, as a result of which Weisz lost £2,000. Bearing Barrie's warning in mind, Weisz refused to pay. There was a row and Weisz left, threatening to call in Scotland Yard. Instead of doing this he consulted ex-Chief Inspector 'Tricky' Drew, who had been involved in most of the leading Turf cases in the preceding twenty years or so, and who was then practising as a private enquiry agent. Drew told him not to pay, explaining that Marsh was a known card-sharper and a crook. Weisz then asked Drew about Barrie, and Drew said he would make enquiries. He returned a day or so later saying, astonishingly, that he could find nothing against Barrie. It may here be mentioned that Drew's own reputation in the racing world was not unsullied, and this may have played a part in his giving Barrie a character clearance. Be that as it may, impressed by this and the warning Barrie had given him against Marsh, Weisz now turned to Barrie for advice on betting and racing. He confided to Barrie that he had lost £2,800 in backing Winkle and Barrie told him he had been had. Barrie then gave him some tips, several of which came up, much to Weisz's delight.

More and more Weisz came to lean on Barrie and as a result Barrie easily persuaded him to buy for £400 a half share in a horse of his called D.N.P. Either this horse did not exist at all, or else he was useless, for he failed to appear on the racecourse. When Weisz enquired why the horse did not run Barrie took him to Berg's stables at Epsom. There a horse was pulled out and shown to Weisz as D.N.P. Barrie explained away the fact that the horse was neither entered nor running by saying that they were having trouble with him and were presently treating him for 'soft toes'. Much later Weisz found out that the horse he was shown was not D.N.P. at all.

But Weisz was by now firmly in Barrie's clutches and pre-pared to swallow almost anything Barrie told him. The next step was for Barrie to introduce Lawley to Weisz. This he did, hinting at the same time that Lawley would shortly have a good thing running in a seller at Cheltenham and suggesting that Weisz should buy him in if he gave him the tip. He added that Lawley, besides being a big property owner in Hampstead, was a government official and a 'stuck-up sort of chap', so that it was unlikely he would say very much when they met. Weisz replied that if that was the case Lawley could keep his pride to himself and he would not bother making conversation with him.

Having laid his plans for entering the horse and having him bought in, Barrie had next to contend with the animal itself, for Shining More in no way resembled the description they had given Weatherby's of the fictitious Silver Badge, and the real Shining More's appearance was in any case by now well known on the racecourse. Silver Badge was described in the letter of entry as a brown mare, while Shining More was a bay with a white blaze and a white hind fetlock. However a small matter of identity was unlikely to give a man of Barrie's ingenuity and criminal intent much trouble. Shortly before the race he moved Shining More from Berg's stables at Epsom to Hampstead, where he had stables of his own. There he dyed Shining More all over, applying the dye most heavily on the blaze and the white fetlock. Thus Shining More, bay, became Silver Badge, a brown mare with no visible markings. To alter her appearance further he also pulled and trimmed her tail. This done, the night before

the race he called on Lawley, gave him £10 to cover his
expenses, and told him to meet him at Cheltenham.

When Lawley arrived at the racecourse he could find neither
Barrie nor the horse. Then a 'rough-looking man' came along
leading a heavily-rugged horse with bandages on all four legs.
Barrie was in attendance and he told Lawley this was Silver
Badge. He then said that he had not engaged a jockey and told
Lawley to find one. When Lawley said he did not know how to
go about this Barrie went with him to the weighing-room. On
enquiring there they found that Tom Hulme, a well-known
hurdle race jockey of the day, was without a mount in their race.
Barrie asked him if he would ride Silver Badge for Lawley.
Hulme went to Silver Badge's box and looked at her, asking
Lawley if she could jump. Primed by Barrie, Lawley told him
she had been well schooled and that he could guarantee her
jumping. 'She can jump all right,' Barrie said. 'She has won
Army competitions.'

Hulme agreed to take the ride and went off to change, leaving
Lawley and Barrie in the box. Lawley by then was having
doubts about the mare's ability. When Barrie gave him a pound
to back her with he pointed out that she was sweating and asked
Barrie if he was still confident. 'If you don't think she'll win give
me the money back,' Barrie said. This was enough for Lawley
and off he went to back the mare.

During all this time Weisz had been busy on his own account.
At the trial he swore that he had never heard the name Silver
Badge until ten minutes before the off. This was not only foolish
but palpably untrue, since no fewer than three bookmakers
were able to show that he had backed the mare by telephone
with them on the day of the race. He had backed her fairly
heavily, too, having £25 at starting price with one, and £100
and £50 with each of the other two. On the course itself he tried
to persuade Louis French, a bookmaker in Tattersall's, to lay
him £1,000 to £100 against Silver Badge. French refused, saying
that was too much for him to carry, but he did lay £500 to £50.
Weisz then went to Bennett, another bookmaker, who laid him
£600 to £100 against Silver Badge. Altogether winnings of over
£3,000 were traced to him on the race. Although he denied it in

the witness box later on and attempted to an absurd degree to exaggerate his ignorance of racing, it is clear that he had at this time, well before the race was ever run, agreed to buy Silver Badge at the subsequent selling auction.

In view of Barrie's skill and persuasiveness, however, there must be considerable doubt as to whether Lawley and Weisz knew then — or indeed much later — that Silver Badge existed solely in Barrie's fertile imagination. For Barrie, with typical ingenuity and thoroughness, had taken precautions which might well have deceived far more experienced racing men than Lawley and Weisz. Silver Badge, in terms of her letter of entry which had been accepted by the authorities, was described on the racecard as: 'Aged, bay mare, pedigree unknown, purchased at army sale, Bristol, March 18th 1919.' And, to make assurance doubly sure, Barrie had made a further entry for the real Shining More, 'trained by W. Berg', in the very next race, the 2·45, so that her name also appeared on the racecard with her true description on it. She did not, of course, run.

After Hulme had weighed out he handed the saddle to Lawley who did not appear to know what to do with it. Barrie therefore took it and saddled the mare. In the ring it was Barrie who gave the jockey his instructions. 'She does it in twice,' he said, which Hulme took to mean that she required a breather during the race and would then run on. Barrie also promised him £50 if the mare won.

Naturally enough they did not bring Silver Badge into the ring until the last possible moment. As a result, Hulme said, he barely had time to get to the post. After that he had no worries, for the mare won easily by six lengths. The starting price was 10—1. Barrie admitted afterwards to taking £7,000 out of the ring on this pretty swindle.

But he still had several things to do to tidy up loose ends and cover his tracks. When they were unsaddling he told Hulme that he was rather short of ready money but that he would see he got his £50 in due course. In this, at least, he kept his word and Hulme got a cheque a few weeks afterwards. Then Barrie hurried off to make sure Weisz bought the mare in.

Weisz was on his way to the auction when he met him.

According to Weisz he had not then made up his mind to buy in Silver Badge, but Barrie persuaded him, saying: 'If you buy her in she will certainly win the Chester Cup and very likely the Grand National. Would you like your friends to see you win the Grand Prix at Auteuil?'

Weisz maintained that he was such a racing simpleton he could not see the absurdities of this statement and that he replied: 'Oh, I should love to!' and that Barrie then said: 'Well, then, now's your chance.' At that, Weisz said, he determined to have the mare at any price.

Considerable interest was shown in the mare and there was some competitive bidding. The auctioneer entered into the spirit of things by describing Silver Badge as an unknown Army horse and telling his audience that marks on her shoulder were 'shrapnel wounds'! Eventually she was knocked down to Weisz, in his *nom de course* of Mr Norman, for 510 guineas.

Immediately Barrie hurried her away and brought her back to Berg's stables. There, with the assistance of one of his own men, he tried to remove the dye by washing her all over with petrol. This did not work, so Barrie produced a dozen bottles of peroxide which proved more efficacious, and gradually Silver Badge resumed something approaching her true colour, and became her real self, Shining More.

While all this was going on Berg arrived at the box and, according to him, demanded to know what the hell was going on. Barrie told him he had given the mare a gallop, after which he had put on some 'new American bath wash' while she was hot, and it had changed her colour. Berg said he accepted this explanation and went off.

The following day there was considerable press comment on the mare's win, all of it drawing attention to her unorthodox and fictitious history conjured up by Barrie. Perhaps the most interesting was the *Sporting Life* report:

Silver Badge is a very appropriate name for an Army surplus horse. This big-framed, sound-looking mare who made hacks of her rivals was at the Shirehampton Remount Depot before Mr C. S. Lawley purchased her at the Army sale in Bristol on

March 18th for, it is said, only 19 gns.... After winning she made 510 gns to Mr Norman, the latter, a pearl merchant, being a newcomer to the Turf. She is now to be sent to Goswell to be trained.

She was not, of course, sent to Goswell, and a few days later Weisz took a party of friends down to Berg's stables to admire his new purchase. Silver Badge was not there, but Barrie was. Meeting the party, he explained to Weisz that he had moved Silver Badge to his own stables in Hampstead as she was very nervous and he wanted to get her used to traffic before sending her to Ireland to win a big race.

Weisz swallowed this explanation and returned, disappointed, to London. He went to a jewel sale in Lausanne in the middle of the month and was out of the country until March. He was still delighted with his purchase, however, and still believed in Barrie. He made arrangements for his horses to stay in Barrie's care and management during his absence. He also left instructions with his office that any tips phoned in by Barrie were to be backed, as a result of which, he afterwards claimed, he lost £1,800.

While he was away several developments took place. Spurred on by Weatherby's and the Jockey Club, the CID stepped up their enquiries. The trail they uncovered led them from Coat of Mail at Stockton to Silver Badge at Cheltenham and it became more and more apparent to them that Barrie's was the brain behind both frauds.

Barrie, as it happened, was beginning to plot yet another coup, but first he and Hopkins decided that they must get rid of Coat of Mail, preferably by shipping him out of the country and away from the eyes of the authorities. In February another jockey, Edward Hardie, came from India just as Collis had done, to buy horses to race there. His contract stipulated that he should ship five horses a month. He had known Hopkins for eight years and had dealt with him on and off during that time. Hopkins introduced him to Barrie and the three of them had dinner together at the Queen's Hotel. Over the meal Barrie and Hopkins suggested to Hardie that he should buy Coat of Mail for £1,000. They assured him he was worth every penny of it and produced the relevant copy of the *Racing Calendar* to show how he had won in a canter at Stockton. As a further inducement they added — for a change, this was true — that Griggs, who had ridden him at Stockton, had been so impressed that he had tried to buy the horse from them himself but could not meet the asking price.

Hardie was interested and agreed to go to Berg's stables to look at Coat of Mail. On his way he called first on Hopkins and the two of them drove together to Downs House where Berg trained. On the way Hardie said to Hopkins, 'If this horse Coat of Mail is as good as you say he is why are you letting him go for £1,000?' Hopkins's reply was that Coat of Mail had won so easily that he would be slaughtered by the handicapper if he ran again in England. Therefore he wanted to cash him now and it was a great chance for Hardie to take him to India where his form would not be known.

When they arrived at Downs House, Hopkins said to one of the lads: 'Pull the little horse out.' From the box came what Hardie described as 'a perky little brown horse with a flowing mane'. When he commented that the horse did not seem to resemble the description of Coat of Mail which he had been given, Hopkins said, 'Never mind, he's a flyer,' and the lad who was holding him immediately put in: 'This horse, sir, he could catch pigeons.'

Hopkins then said: 'You know he beat Plymouth Rock six lengths at Stockton and Plymouth Rock was very nearly the best two-year-old last year.'

Convinced by all this, and satisfied that he was getting Coat of Mail at the right price, Hardie agreed to take him. It was not, of course, Coat of Mail that he saw but a horse called Stubble which Berg had actually sold to Gibraltar for £200, having originally purchased him for 70 guineas.

When he returned to London Hardie, fortunately for himself, ran into Bowley, the friend to whom Collis had poured out his woes about Coat of Mail. Bowley warned Hardie to be very careful in any dealings about the horse. After thinking things over, Hardie rang Hopkins and told him he had heard things about Coat of Mail and had decided not to take him.

Hopkins said: 'You've been listening to rumours,' and when Hardie agreed that he had, Hopkins went on: 'If they say any more to you take it down in black and white, and get them to sign it and see what I will do.' Hardie, however, refused to change his mind and to take the horse.

So Barrie and Hopkins still had Coat of Mail on their hands and, though this was not at the moment so serious, Shining More too. But then a further complication ensued. Weisz returned to England, examined his betting accounts, found he had lost nearly £2,000, mostly on backing Barrie's tips, and he, too, heard rumours and paid heed to them. In Weisz's case the rumours concerned Shining More and Silver Badge. Weisz resolved to go to Barrie and have the matter out with him. The encounter took place at Downs House. At first Barrie flew into a rage and threatened to knock the block off the man who had told things to Weisz. After a little while he calmed down and said to Weisz: 'Mr Weisz, how can you be such an ass as to believe rumours of that kind? You saw the horse at Cheltenham. Cheltenham is the home of horsey people. Shining More is a veteran race winner. It has won nine or ten races and is as well-known to these racing men as a champion boxer or famous footballer would be to you. It is a few low-class bookmakers who lost heavily and are annoyed who are putting these rumours about. That sort of thing is always happening in racing.'

Barrie was a plausible and convincing liar. This speech so took the wind out of Weisz's sails that he made Barrie a grovelling apology for daring to suggest that there might have been anything suspect about Silver Badge's running. He did, however, ask where the mare was now. Barrie told him she had broken down while in training in Ireland and was still there and suggested that the best thing to do was to breed from her. After sympathizing with Weisz on his bad luck over the mare Barrie suggested that he should buy Shining More who was, he said, bound to win races and recover all his losses for him.

Weisz, once more completely bemused and taken in, agreed. A most complicated transaction then took place which ended up with Weisz giving Barrie a cheque for £350 and becoming the owner of Shining More. Then Barrie presented him with a bill for £92 covering training fees for Silver Badge, which Weisz also paid without hesitation. Weisz had now become the proud owner of a mare he had paid for twice and the person responsible for training fees on an animal that did not exist! Before the bubble burst Shining More did get something back for him for she ran in his name at Manchester and won, netting him £1,250.

As has been said, while all this was going on Barrie was hatching yet another scheme, almost identical with that which had proved so successful with Coat of Mail. Again he invented a fictitious owner and a non-existent horse. Before the closing of entries for the Wynn two-year-old selling plate at Chester to be run on 6 May he made an entry in it for a colt, Golden Plate, by Prospector out of Lady Maer, the property of J. H. Hawkins of 28 Bruton Place, Berkeley Square. Horse, owner's name, fashionable address, even the breeding, as a quick check by Weatherby's would have shown, were all false. Nevertheless the entry was accepted without question.

Some time before the race was due to be run Barrie and Berg went to Stanley Wootton's stable and purchased a three-year-old called Homs for £350, telling Wootton that they wanted him for a friend to race abroad. Homs was sent to Berg's stable and was notified to Weatherby's by Wootton as a sale to Barrie. Berg, being unable to find the £350 himself or obtain it from Barrie, borrowed it from Weisz.

The next step was to get the colt to Chester in such a way that neither Barrie nor Berg would appear to be connected with it. They paid a visit to a neighbouring farmer called Gray who had horses running at Chester. Berg told Gray that he was going abroad and could not therefore look after the horse at Chester. He added that the horse belonged to a wealthy American and that if all went well the American was likely to give Gray other horses to train since he, Berg, was likely to be away for some time. Never one to let a good story go without dressing it up a bit, Barrie added that he knew Hawkins well, that the horse was coming over from Ireland where at the moment it was being trained privately and had been entered as such. After some discussion Gray agreed, so Barrie gave him £15 for his expenses and an authority to act signed by the fictitious J. H. Hawkins.

In all innocence Gray carried out his instructions, travelling up in the train from Euston with Barrie, who asked him to engage a jockey and to give him £25 if Golden Plate won and £10 if he got into the money. Gray booked Tommy Weston, then still an apprentice.

All should have been well, since as a three-year-old Homs ought to have been giving 29lb to the rest of the field at weight-for-age at that time of year, he had been got ready for the race, and they had one of the best of the younger jockeys riding him. But this time things went disastrously wrong for the conspirators. Golden Plate was drawn on the extreme outside, a pretty hopeless position in a five-furlong race at Chester. Also, under his real name, Homs, he may not have been as good as they had thought. In any event, even the fraudulent advantage of the weights added to the apprentice's claim were insufficient to enable him to overcome the unfavourable draw. He ran badly and finished nowhere. Gray was so unimpressed with the horse and his running that he told Barrie he would not train him for a rich American or anyone else, and insisted on Berg taking him back.

Barrie and Berg were now in an unenviable position. The coup had not come off and they now had two fictitious horses — Silver Badge and Golden Plate — on their hands. Despite their well-laid plans they had been unable to spirit them out of the country or rid themselves of them in any other way. Moreover the names of the two horses were now known to both Weatherby's and the Jockey Club and were on their books.

In carrying out these frauds Barrie had seen and exploited a glaring weakness in the application of the rules and the organization of racing at the time. At this point it is worthwhile interpolating the cross-examination of Messrs Weatherby's witness by Berg's counsel at the trial. 'Why was Golden Plate allowed to run at Chester?' he asked. 'If your rules had been carried out this fraud could not have happened, could it?'

To this perfectly plain question he received an evasive and unconvincing reply: 'It would not be Weatherby's business to stop a horse running. It should not run but it would not be grounds for disqualification if it did. The trainer would be asked to explain, and it would be for the stewards to deal with him at their discretion, either by fining him or by making him disqualified.'

'Could I get an old bus horse and enter it for the Derby by simply filling up a form at your office?'

'The Derby is a race for three-year-olds,' the witness replied, avoiding the issue once more, but here the judge intervened: 'Assume the bus horse had the qualification?' he asked.

'I hardly think you could, because horses competing in the Derby are pretty well canvassed beforehand.'

'That is no answer,' counsel said sternly. 'I want to know whose duty it is on a course on behalf of the Jockey Club to see that frauds of this sort are not committed. Take the bus horse I mentioned. Is there anything to prevent my entering it and running it at Stockton or Manchester.

Once more the answer was evasive: 'You would want a licence to ride.'

'If I engaged a jockey?'

The witness was still stalling: 'Your horse would need a name and pedigree,' he said.

'We will give him one as "Mr Hawkins" did.'

'I suppose you could then.'

There it was, out in the open at last for all to see. Barrie had played merry hell with the authorities on three occasions, repeating much the same fraud each time, and had nearly got away with it. However his recklessness and audacity had carried him too far. He had repeated his scheme once too often. Talk was now rampant in racing and elsewhere and the net was closing in.

Early in June Detective-Inspector Gillard called at Hopkins's stables and asked to see Coat of Mail; he also enquired about his age. From there he went on to Downs House where he wanted both Homs and Shining More to be produced for him. This could not be done, for immediately after the Chester race Berg had paid a visit to Brussels, taking both horses with him. Once there he had, he said, handed them over to Weisz's agent on

Weisz's instructions and their further whereabouts were unknown to him.

Nevertheless the enquiries proceeded and on Saturday 6 June
Barrie was arrested on the platform of Charing Cross Station as
he was leaving the Hastings train in the company of his wife. At
first he thought he was being charged with something quite
different and asked: 'Has Captain Norrie got this warrant
against me?' When it was explained to him that the charge
concerned Coat of Mail and Shining More he said: 'I know
nothing whatever about it. I am a man of the world. It looks like
a long job and if you can do anything to help me I shall be
grateful.'

Over the next few weeks Hopkins, Berg, Weisz, Lawley and
Collis were all arrested and charged with being implicated
in one or the other of the frauds. The trial opened before
Mr Justice Greer at the Old Bailey on 13 September 1920.
There was an immediate sensation for Barrie pleaded guilty to
all the charges against him and was taken down to the cells to
await sentence. All the other defendants entered pleas of not
guilty.

The defences of Hopkins and Berg were that they were
innocent parties throughout who had acted in good faith and
had been led astray by Barrie. In Berg's case, apart from the
running of Golden Plate at Chester there was little except
suspicion, grave though it might have been, to implicate him.
Weisz and Lawley both put forward the case that they were
innocent dupes, Weisz doing so with considerable vehemence
and force of expression from the witness box which gained him
little credit with either judge or jury.

When Hopkins went into the box he virtually convicted
himself out of his own mouth and his evidence was so absurd
that it is worth quoting some of it.

'You seem to have been made a dupe, deceived?' prosecuting
counsel, the formidable C. F. Gill KC, asked him.

'Yes, by Barrie.'

'What the witnesses Weisz, Hardie and Persse have sworn
is untrue?'

'It is all untrue.'

197

'Well, let us see what we can agree on. It was a very gross fraud, was it not?'

'Yes, certainly, a disgraceful fraud.'

'You were out of the country when the Stockton meeting took place, you told us, but is it not the case that you had a bet with Mr Ike White at the Sandown meeting on the same day?'

'Yes, £10. It was put on for me by a friend. It was on a horse called Knock in a hurdle.'

'Did you look to see if it won?'

'I did.'

'Did you look at the results of the Stockton meeting?'

'No. I was not interested in the flat race meeting. I was looking for the hurdle race at Sandown.'

'So at no time did you see that your horse Coat of Mail had won at Stockton?'

'No.'

'You did not see the headlines "The Stockton Coup Comes Off", "Easy for Coat of Mail"?'

'No. It would be quite easy to see the report of one meeting and miss the other.'

'When did you first hear the rumours that Jazz had been substituted for Coat of Mail?'

'Sometime in April.'

'Did you consult the *Racing Calendar* to check up on it?'

'Not then but I did later. I found that Coat of Mail started favourite and won by six lengths.'

'And all the time the poor horse was sick in your stable?'

'Yes.'

'And not in training so that no sporting writer could know anything about it?'

'Yes.'

'Wasn't the result of the race in every newspaper in the country?'

'I don't know. I never read the newspapers. I'm too busy.'

At this point the judge intervened. 'What did you say to Barrie when you discovered the fraud?' he asked.

'I didn't know Barrie had had anything to do with it until he was arrested,' was the reply.

'How many men do you employ?'

'Four, m'lord.'

'They all know you had Coat of Mail?'

'Yes.'

'Did any one of them ever say to you that he had seen that Coat of Mail had won this race?'

'Never, my lord.'

'You have many friends who visit your stables and would know you had Coat of Mail?'

'They would know it by name.'

'Did anyone congratulate you on having won this race?'

'They would not know it was mine then. I sell my horses which win a few days afterwards.'

'Your answer is that you were not congratulated,' was the judge's dry comment on that reply.

The unfortunate Lawley, who was to some extent a dupe, admitted in the box that he had received the stake money on Silver Badge's win.

'What happened to it?' counsel asked him.

'Barrie persuaded me to pay £100 for a share in another horse, Rotterdam. I suppose it was his way of getting hold of the stake money. I have never to this day seen the horse.'

'That was £100 out of the £189. What happened to the rest?'

'In the train, on the way back from the races, Barrie introduced me to a bookmaker friend of his and we played cards. The bookmaker said he didn't understand the game.'

'Did he win?'

'I don't know. I only know I lost!'

'Did you know that Weisz won £3,000 on your horse?'

'I did not know that. I had no particular interest in Weisz. Barrie was always boasting about him as his friend the American millionaire. If I'd known that I'd certainly have had a bottle of wine from him.'

'How much did you win on the race?'

'I had the £1 Barrie had given me and I asked a friend to put a tenner on for me. I won about £200.'

'So it was a good day for you,' the judge said.

'I thought so then. As a matter of fact it was about the worst day I ever had,' was the rueful reply, and here, certainly, Lawley spoke the truth.

As one man the bookies rallied to Weisz's defence. Barnett, the man to whom he had given the pearl pin, came out perhaps most strongly on his behalf. 'He is one of my best punters,' Barnett said.

'Did he usually win or lose?'

'He more often lost.'

'That is why you call him one of your best punters?'

'Yes, and I am sure he did not know anything about cheating because he told me if he found he had had money from me dishonestly he would give it back.'

Lew French, the man who had refused to lay Weisz £1,000—£100, also testified to his sterling character. 'I saw him at Lingfield shortly after his return from abroad,' he said. 'I asked him how Silver Badge was getting on and he threatened to sue me for libel.'

'What did you say to that?'

'I said I'd heard rumours about Silver Badge but I still said Silver Badge was a good horse.'

'I don't suppose he threatened to sue you for that. Did he add anything else?'

'Yes, he said he had never taken a dishonourable bet in his life and if anything was wrong he would return the money. I always found him a most honourable man, he has a good reputation on the Turf and he is still betting with me.'

Despite all this there was, to say the least of it, considerable suspicion attaching to Weisz. In addition to his actions over Silver Badge — backing him heavily and buying him in — he was in some way concerned with the purchase of Homs, for it was his money which had paid for the horse. Also Berg had sworn that it was to his agent that he had handed over both Homs and Shining More in Belgium when things began to look really nasty for them all. A mixture of stupidity, cupidity, and ambition to become a personage on the Turf had put him in the dock with the rest.

The trial lasted nineteen days. Barrie, having pleaded guilty, was given three years' hard labour, a light enough sentence in the circumstances. Hopkins was convicted on all charges brought against him, given fifteen months' imprisonment without hard labour, and ordered to pay the costs of the prosecution. Berg was lucky. He was convicted only in the affair of Homs and received nine months' imprisonment without hard labour.

Weisz was found guilty in the Silver Badge case, sentenced to fifteen months in the second division and ordered to pay the costs of his prosecution. His counsel promptly applied for and was given leave to appeal.* Lawley, the comparative innocent, was found guilty only of receiving the stake money in Silver Badge's race. The jury in so finding added a rider that his part in the whole affair had been a subordinate one, and he escaped with a fine of £100. In the case of Collis the jury again stressed that he only came into the Coat of Mail case after the race had been run, and he was bound over in his own recognizances of £100 and one surety of £100.

So ended one of the most sensational of all trials concerning the running of ringers. Barrie's schemes were ingenious, well thought out, and were marred only by his extreme audacity which reached the point of recklessness, and, of course, the weakness of all such schemes, that the accomplices must hold their tongues, which they did not. Once the secret is out, then, in Barrie's own words in his statement, 'There will be a tumble.' But Barrie spoke the truth when he told Collis: 'It is easy to run a ringer in this country.'

The honour of the Turf, as *The Times* pronounced in a leading article after the case, may have been preserved by the trial and conviction of the leading players in these frauds, but at least some blame must be attached to an administration which permitted their blatant perpetration with apparent immunity for so long.

---

* Weisz's appeal failed as did that of Barrie. Hopkins was luckier — his sentence of hard labour was commuted to fifteen months in the second division.

CHAPTER 10

Derby Day 1934: The Race
Colombo Did Not Win

IT ALL STARTED, as so many things did in the racing world in that era, with Steve Donoghue. Charming, feckless, arguably the best horseman who ever sat in a racing saddle, irresponsible beyond the point of foolishness where obligations to owners and trainers were concerned, in 1934 he had reached the age of fifty leaving behind him a whole history of broken contracts, retainers thrown aside and engagements evaded, together with an assortment of wrathful and disappointed owners, some of them the greatest in the land.

As early as 1920 he had been a party to the 'jocking off', to use the modern expression, of Jellis from the well-fancied Abbott's Trace in order to get himself the ride in the Derby of that year. In 1921 he displeased Lord Derby and his trainer, George Lambton, by wheedling and charming his way out of Lord Derby's retainer in order to take the mount on the fancied Humorist for Mr J. B. Joel. On Humorist he rode possibly the best of his many great races to win the Derby, but the following year he lost Lord Derby's retainer and with it the possibility of riding two future Derby winners in Sansovino and Hyperion. Once more in 1922 he was concerned in yet another 'jocking off', to enable him to take the ride on Captain Cuttle, this time for Lord Woolavington. But again the Woolavington connection did not last, for he let down the enormously rich and powerful whisky baron the following season by deserting his

202

Derby runners — and breaking his retainer — in order to ride the well-backed Papyrus on which he won, giving him three Derby winners in a row. Although the formidable Fred Darling, having observed these manoeuvres, refused him a retainer, he did not object to one of his owners, Mr Morris making an independent arrangement with Steve to ride Manna in 1925. Manna won, and thus gave Steve four Derby victories in five years. He was a public figure and a public favourite. The cry 'Come on Steve' echoed round every racetrack in England. The story that he told King George V's racing manager: 'I should like to ride for His Majesty, my Lord, but I'm afraid his horses aren't good enough,' may be apocryphal but certainly then the whole world seemed to be at his feet.

In fact the great days were over. He had been up to his tricks once too often; he was not quite as young as he had been and the charm was wearing thin. Owners, and especially the more powerful ones, were wary of him. Do what he would, as year succeeded year he could not win his way back into their favour.

In 1933 Steve, the greatest Epsom rider of his time, was actually without a mount in the Derby. At the usual pre-race luncheon Lord Derby, hearing this, with his accustomed kindliness offered him the ride on his second string, Thrapston. Lord Derby's first runner was the immortal Hyperion on whom Tommy Weston, the then stable jockey, had the ride which might indeed have been Steve's had he honoured his obligations back in the 1920s.

In effect Thrapston was all but a pacemaker for Hyperion. At Tattenham Corner Steve was in his accustomed place glued to the rails with Hyperion tracking him. Thrapston was obviously beaten and both Donoghue and Weston knew it. 'Get out of the way and let a bloody racehorse come by,' Weston shouted. Steve at once obligingly pulled out. Hyperion slipped through the gap and went on to win easily by three lengths from King Salmon.

All these things had a bearing on what was to happen in 1934. By then Steve had reached fifty, was nearing retirement and was desperately anxious to rehabilitate himself by riding another Derby winner before he hung up his boots. And during 1933 he had made up his mind that he had a very good chance of doing so.

Lord Glanely had been born William James Tathem in a small town in Devon. As a young man he went to sea and worked in a shipping office. Clever, industrious and ambitious, he fought his way to the top, accumulated wealth and founded his own shipping line. In 1909 he entered racing and enjoyed some small success. In 1918, in reward for services during the war, he was created a peer, and in the following year won the Derby with Grand Parade. His outlay on yearlings during the 1920s was prodigious and mostly ill-advised, rivalling that of Miss Dorothy Paget a decade later. But Grand Parade only cost him 470 guineas and in 1932 he secured another bargain when he paid 510 guineas for a colt by Manna out of Lady Nairne whom he called Colombo.

'Old Guts and Gaiters', to give him the name by which he was irreverently and affectionately known to the racing public, may have squandered money on yearlings but he could be cheese-paring with his jockeys and fickle, too, about whom he employed. At the end of the 1931 season he lost his first claim on Gordon Richards through trying, most unreasonably, to cut the amount of the retainer. As a result Richards went to Beckhampton as first jockey to Fred Darling where he would achieve brilliant success as the racing records show. But Glanely, having lost him, persistently tried to persuade him to return. Richards just as persistently refused, but he did continue to ride for him when he was not claimed elsewhere.

When Colombo started his racing career as a two-year-old Lord Glanely had no jockey retained. Colombo had a difficult temperament and had been troublesome to break, and when Captain Hogg, who had now become Lord Glanely's private trainer, started to work him he proved a far from easy ride. Knowing that Steve was down on his luck and knowing also what a beautiful horseman he was, Hogg asked him to ride Colombo in one of his early gallops. The colt went beautifully for Donoghue and made a great impression on him.

Richards, however, had the mount on Colombo in five of the colt's two-year-old races. Because he was claimed elsewhere

Donoghue was given the ride on him when he won the Richmond Stakes at Goodwood and, his last race of the season, the Imperial Produce Stakes at Kempton. Colombo wound up the season unbeaten and headed the Free Handicap with 9st 7lb.

Donoghue, probably better than any other jockey in history except Archer or Piggott, could 'sense' a Derby winner when he sat on its back and he was convinced that Colombo would win not only next year's Derby but the Triple Crown as well. He was sure that Richards would be claimed by Beckhampton and so he persuaded himself that he would be offered the Derby ride. So certain was he of this that he did not indulge in any of his usual wheeling and dealing about the ride nor did he make any direct approach to Lord Glanely, but in his happy-go-lucky way went off at the end of the season on a holiday to South America without leaving a forwarding address.

Although Colombo, after his brilliant two-year-old career, was being built up almost everywhere as the natural successor to the greatest horses of the past, not everyone agreed with these inflated opinions. Lady Nairne, his dam, had produced nothing of any account and it was held in some quarters that on his breeding he might not stay a mile and a half in top-class company in a fast run race. Lord Glanely himself had not been impressed by his last victory, when it had seemed to him that his colt had only just scraped home from the indifferent Valerius to whom he was giving 17lb. It seems that Glanely was uncertain whether to blame the horse or the rider for this result. Donoghue had assured him that he could have won as he liked, and had only done so 'cleverly' so as not to give the colt a hard race after his long season and to send him happy into winter quarters.

In this Donoghue, who had wonderful sympathy with all horses, was almost certainly right but 'Old Guts and Gaiters', who had not much sympathy with either horses or men, apparently had at the back of his mind the memory of Donoghue letting him down when riding a horse of his years ago in the Cesarewitch and the fear that he might do so again. If he believed he had been shopped by Donoghue he was almost certainly wrong, for it is universally accepted that when Steve rode in a big race he rode to win, and no inducement would be large enough to make him do otherwise.

Despite his doubts, Glanely did make an attempt to get in touch with Steve with a view to discussing plans for the next season, only to find that no one knew just where he was, no letters were being forwarded and nothing had been heard from him since he left England. Glanely cannot therefore have been exactly mollified to learn via the press that the jockey had apparently pre-empted his decision, when answering a question from a South American reporter as to what would win next year's Derby, by saying: 'Colombo with myself in the saddle.'

Whether it was this rash answer that finally swung the scales against Steve no one now can say, but unquestionably around this time Lord Glanely decided that he must look elsewhere for a jockey. And at this point another actor comes on to the scene. William Raphael (Rae) Johnstone was an Australian from New South Wales. Apprenticed at the age of fourteen, he was riding winners before he was out of his indentures and success came to him quickly. A born and compulsive gambler with a love of the limelight, and driven on the racecourse by an all-consuming urge to win, he did not endear himself to the authorities. His early career was stormy and he suffered several suspensions. Wanderlust had him in its grip, too — he wanted to see the world and to conquer it. During a spell in India he was offered the rides in England on Sir Victor Sassoon's horses and accepted.

Steve was then riding for Sir Victor. The two men shared a taste for the bright lights, gambling and the good life. They became firm friends and Johnstone, much the younger of the two, conceived something approaching hero-worship for Steve.

Johnstone, who admits himself that at this period of his life success was a wine he could not carry, had come to England certain that he had the racing world at his feet. It was therefore a considerable blow to him when the Jockey Club stewards refused him a licence to ride. The stewards were not obliged to give any reasons for their refusal, nor did they, save the singularly unconvincing one that they were not granting any new licences at that time. Johnstone, however, was convinced and indeed was told on the grapevine that it was because of his unruly record in Australia. In the meantime he was stranded in England, passing his days mostly in Steve's company, travelling about with him, learning something of the idiosyncrasies of the various tracks and watching him ride. More and more he fell under the spell of the famous charm and was entranced with Steve's skills in the saddle. When Steve went to Paris to ride in the Grand Prix Johnstone accompanied him and while there, out of the blue, he received an offer to ride the Wertheimer horses.

As the records show, Johnstone was a really great jockey. He loved to ride a waiting race, which earned him the nickname from the French public of *'Le Crocodil'* because, they said, he came on the scene late and ate up the other horses. Long ago, in Australia, he had had another nickname, 'Togo', which he hated and which sprang from his Oriental cast of features. He certainly had something of the Oriental impassivity for his face remained unchanging and inscrutable through triumph and disaster. This, coupled with an original sense of humour drily and tersely expressed, did not serve him well in the Derby sensation which was soon to erupt.

In France Johnstone headed the jockeys' list in 1933 with eighty-eight winners but he ran into some trouble with the authorities there, too, chiefly due to his ruthlessness in coming through from behind in his determination to win. During this time his friendship with Steve continued; he had a few rides in England on a temporary licence, one of them being in the Derby of 1933 on an outsider, Melfort, trained by Frank Hartigan.

Melfort finished well down the field in the Derby, and that was Johnstone's sole experience of Epsom. But his fame had spread. His record in France spoke for itself. His reputation as a judge of pace, a horseman and above all a jockey who meant to win, appealed to Lord Glanely. In the winter of 1933 feelers were put out to ascertain if he would accept Lord Glanely's retainer to ride his horses during the coming season in England. These horses included, of course, Colombo, who was regarded as a certainty for both the Guineas and the Derby and being backed accordingly. In his memoirs Johnstone says

207

Colombo 'had all the appearance of being the racing machine of the era'. He accepted without hesitation.

When the news broke and Steve heard of it on his return to England he was furious. He had confidently expected that he would be given the ride on Colombo, and now here was Lord Glanely offering the ride behind his back — so he thought and said — to an outsider, an Australian, one who had made his name Down Under, in India and France, and had little or no experience of English racetracks and above all of Epsom.

Steve had no possible justification for his anger and resentment, for he had no claim whatsoever on Lord Glanely's bounty or his retainer. But all his life, regrettably, where fancied rides were concerned he was a spoilt child and like a spoilt child he convinced himself that what he wanted was his by right.

Johnstone, of course, knew nothing of this. When he arrived in England, after being handed a cheque for £1,000 by his employer 'to help him acclimatize himself and settle in', he took a flat in St John's Wood and looked up his old pal, Steve. For once Steve appears to have concealed his feelings, at least from Johnstone if from no one else, and their friendship was resumed. They were seen about town together enjoying the bright lights at all the most fashionable watering-places of the day.

So far as racing was concerned, although Lord Glanely's two-year-olds did not come up to Johnstone's expectations he and Colombo got off to a great start. At his first outing of the season Colombo won the Craven Stakes in a manner that seemed to stamp him all over a champion. Once again, however, there were some murmurs among the cognoscenti that he had beaten nothing. Not all of these doubters had their fears put at rest by the result of the Two Thousand Guineas. Colombo, starting at 7—2 on, the shortest-priced Guineas favourite since St Frusquin in 1896, won it all right but he seemed to some people to have been extended in doing so. For the first time since his very early days he showed signs of temperament and sweated up in the parade ring. He had settled down at the start and jumped immediately into his stride. At the bushes, though, he had faltered and Johnstone had had to show him the whip before he ran on to beat the French horse, Easton, by a neck. Johnstone's comment afterwards, a strange one in view of what was to happen on Derby Day and the views expressed by experts on that race, was, 'The impression I got was that he had won *by staying.*' (Johnstone's own italics.)

At all events, that, for the moment, was that. Colombo's next race was to be the Derby. Public confidence in him, only momentarily shaken, was restored by the news that he was working well at home. He continued to be backed like a certainty for the big one.

In the meantime at Lambourn a young trainer called Marcus Marsh was quietly bringing on another colt to peak fitness before the Derby. Marsh, who until recently had been assistant trainer to Fred Darling, had brought Windsor Lad as a yearling in 1932 for £1,300 Guineas on behalf of the Maharajah of Rajpipla. As a classic prospect no fault could be found in his breeding, for he was by Blandford out of Resplendent who had won the Irish One Thousand Guineas and Oaks and run second in the Oaks at Epsom.

Marsh at that time ran a comparatively small stable and Windsor Lad did not have a particularly distinguished career as a two-year-old. He had three outings, the last of which had been his only win in the six-furlong Criterion Stakes at Newmarket. In the Free Handicap he was rated at 8st 3lb — 18lb behind Colombo.

There was no ballyhoo at all about Windsor Lad or his preparation, but he won the Chester Vase and the Newmarket Stakes, his only two outings before the Derby. In the latter race he was ridden by Charlie Smirke who had only recently 'come in from the cold' after a five-year suspension for his riding of a horse called Welcome Gift, a sentence almost universally considered to have been unjustified.

By a coincidence Johnstone had himself later ridden Welcome Gift in India. He had very nearly got into trouble with the Calcutta stewards over the horse's crazy antics. He called him a 'heartbreak horse' and refused to ride him again.

Smirke was never one to hide his or his horse's chances under a bushel. He had formed a high opinion of Windsor Lad from the moment he first rode him. Full of confidence as he always was about his mount in a big race, and not slow to express it, he warned Johnstone when they met at Chester and Johnstone replied laughingly that Windsor Lad might give him a nice lead into the straight at Epsom: 'He'll lead you all right, Rae. All the way.'

Things were happening, too, at Beckhampton. Fred Darling had come to the conclusion that his one-time Derby prospect, Mediaeval Knight, was not of classic quality, and he purchased Easton, whom Colombo had so narrowly defeated in the Guineas, for Lord Woolavington at, it was said, £15,000. Gordon Richards as first jockey would have the mount on Easton. Darling, however, was determined to run Mediaeval Knight as well so as to ensure that the gallop, to suit Easton, would be a good one. He had no jockey for Mediaeval Knight, and he looked around for one.

Just what Steve was up to in the few weeks before the Derby no one knows. Outwardly he and Johnstone were still on the friendliest of terms, with Johnstone constantly in and out of Steve's luxurious chambers in Albany. Inwardly we do know — for he has said so himself — that he was seething with disappointment and resentment. He approached Lord Glanely and tried all the famous wheedling charm to persuade him to stand down Johnstone and to give him the ride on Colombo. It had worked before but his escapades at the expense of owners, his comings and goings, his history of contracts torn up and retainers set aside had at long last earned its recompense. 'Old Guts and Gaiters' was adamant. Johnstone had the retainer and he would have the ride.

Hearing that Steve was free, Darling offered him the mount on Mediaeval Knight. Disgusted, Donoghue nevertheless accepted. So, for the second successive year, the great Epsom jockey was reduced to playing the humble rôle of pacemaker.

It has been suggested that Steve played on his friendship with Johnstone and on Johnstone's hero-worship and his confidence in Steve's knowledge of the best way to ride the tricky Derby course. 'Track me and you will be all right' is what it is believed in some quarters Donoghue said to him — and this with malice aforethought, for

Donoghue knew Mediaeval Knight had stamina limitations.

If Steve did all this he acted quite out of character, for he was not a man to bear grudges and to hatch a plot of this kind would be utterly foreign to his nature. But he was ageing, he was in financial difficulties, he had been in the wilderness or something approaching it for too long, and his one last chance of crowning his career had been unfairly, or so he had persuaded himself, swept away from him.

On the great day confidence in Colombo was undiminished. He was backed steadily down to 11—8 against, the hottest Derby favourite for years. Lord Glanely had already stated that he believed Colombo to be a great horse and the only thing which could beat him was bad luck. To underline his belief, before he left for the races he ordered his favourite restaurateur to prepare a celebration dinner in anticipation of his triumphant return. To say the least of it, this smacked of the kind of hubris racing rarely forgives.

In the parade ring Colombo looked lean and hard and trained to the minute, but once again he showed signs of temperament. He began to sweat up and some observers noted a tell-tale bump between the eyes which could denote a lack of generosity if things did not go all his own way. Windsor Lad, on the other hand, a tougher, bulkier sort than the favourite, was as calm as could be and the testing Derby preliminaries bothered him not at all. There was considerable stable confidence behind him, too, and he was well backed at 15—2.

In a very high-class field both Johnstone and Smirke had summed up the dangers — apart from each other — as Easton, ridden by Gordon Richards, Umwidwar with Harry Wragg in the saddle, and Mediaeval Knight, representing the incalculable and unpredictable since he was ridden by Steve, who might well produce a touch of pure magic from somewhere. Mediaeval Knight had won the Lingfield Derby Trial which had persuaded Johnstone he would stay, but Smirke had marked him down as 'a quitter'.

The pressures on Johnstone that day were immense. He was riding the favourite, a horse who had been built up as all but unbeatable, stories were going round which he must have heard that the English jockeys resented his presence on Colombo and would not let him win, and the precedent of Reiff being brought over from France to ride Craganour and what happened to him cannot have been reassuring. To cap it all he had, he says, some days before, been offered £10,000 to stop Colombo.

As in the Guineas, Colombo had settled by the time they reached the starting-gate. There was no delay and the moment the tapes went up Steve pushed Mediaeval Knight into the lead on the rails with Johnstone tracking him. Behind Johnstone but more out towards the centre of the course were Smirke on Windsor Lad and Richards on Easton.

At Tattenham Corner the order was much the same. Then, as so often happens just there in the Derby, things began to happen very quickly indeed. Mediaeval Knight began to hang out distress signals. Smirke, whose reactions were more nearly instantaneous than those of any other jockey then riding, and who had in any event anticipated something of the sort, saw his opportunity and took it. He slipped past Mediaeval Knight, followed by Richards on Easton.

Johnstone, who realized what was happening to Mediaeval Knight a fraction of a second too late, was by then boxed in by a wall of horses. There was nothing he could do but sit and suffer until he could pull out and make his run on the outside. The instant the opportunity arose, he did so.

Colombo answered him with tremendous courage. He got to Easton's girths, held him and then started to wear him down. But Windsor Lad had got first run and was gone beyond recall. He passed the post a length ahead of Easton who, in turn, only held off Colombo by a neck. And then, of course, the inquests and the recriminations began.

One of the first things widely said was that the English jockeys had ganged up on Johnstone and stopped him. Johnstone himself disposed of that with one laconic word — 'bunk'. But it was accepted then, as it has been ever since, by most critics that Johnstone, by following Steve and allowing himself to be shut in, rode an atrociously bad race. Steve himself wrote afterwards: 'Mark you, had he called out to me to let him through when I realized I was whacked, I would, of course, have let him through. . . .' Quinney Gilbey, the well-known racing writer who knew all the actors in this drama personally, made the aptest comment on this statement when he wrote: 'Like hell he would!' Nor, indeed, was there any obligation whatever on Steve to pull out and let the favourite up. But Gilbey goes on to voice the surely controversial opinion that the check did Colombo good, not harm, since as a non-stayer it 'gave him the breather he so badly needed'.

Perhaps Gilbey was right, but what evidence was there or is there that Colombo was a non-stayer? Johnstone himself says he won the Guineas like a stayer and puts the statement in italics in his book. And he was catching Easton hand over fist at the line despite coming round a wall of horses. It should, however, be added that after the Derby Johnstone, arguing from events, says he became convinced that Colombo did not stay. The kindest and probably truest comment on Johnstone's riding came from a fellow jockey, Freddy Fox: 'He stayed on the rails just too long,' he said.

During all the hullabaloo following Johnstone's defeat and the barrage of questions he had to face from the press the jockey's features retained their accustomed Oriental impassivity. It was this which gave rise to the allegation which ran like wildfire round the racecourse in the course of the afternoon that he did not care whether he won or not. And when cornered outside the weighing-room by Hannen Swaffer, a muck-raking journalist of the day, he did not help his own cause by his terse remark to him: 'At any rate no lives were lost!'

The fact that he did not ride Colombo must have indeed rankled with Steve, for in his reminiscences, written four years later when one might have expected someone of his resilient and ebullient character to have mellowed, he wrote: 'Had I ridden him [Colombo] he would have won, on the bit, by lengths. He would have had an easy race and a decisive victory.' He may have been right, for the 'non-staying' theories were never put to the test. In any event the Derby has been won before and since by non-stayers through brilliance of jockeyship. Colombo's next outing was the St James's Palace Stakes at Royal Ascot. There, starting at odds of 5—1 on, he was beaten by Flamenco whom he had slammed in the Guineas. This race, over a mile, really proved nothing for it is almost certain that his hard race in the Derby was still having its effect on him. He was then trained for the St Leger for which he was well backed in the ante-post market but he injured himself in preparation and was retired to stud.

Lord Glanely appears to have vacillated between the view that Steve had 'done' Colombo and stopped him from winning and that Johnstone had thrown the race away. Relations between Johnstone and 'Old Guts and Gaiters' were never the same after the race. In mid-season, by mutual agreement, the contract giving Johnstone the retainer was rescinded and the jockey returned to France. Before he left the English flat race scene his fellow jockeys clubbed together to give him a dinner at the Piccadilly Hotel. It looked like a sporting gesture to one whose race-riding career, so far as England was concerned, was over forever. At the airport a reporter asked him: 'Any final word on Colombo?'

'Yes,' Johnstone answered: 'If he'd been ridden in the Derby by a jockey, he'd have won ten minutes.' Though he spoke sardonically and in jest that opinion was echoed by most of the pundits. It was said that he would never make a Derby jockey.

Yet after the war he was triumphantly to prove them all wrong for he rode three winners of the Derby (and was perhaps unlucky not to have ridden a fourth) and the same number of the Oaks. It was noticeable, all the same, that in all these victories he did not hug the rails, preferring to preserve his freedom of action by keeping to the centre of the course. The lesson of 1934 had been learnt the hard way.

Bibliography

WILLIAM ALLISON *My Kingdom For A Horse* London 1919
  Memories of Men and Horses London 1922
ANONYMOUS *Illustrated Life and Career of William Palmer of Rugeley*
  London 1867
ERNEST BLAND (Editor) *Flat-Racing Since 1900* London 1950
J. B. BOOTH *Old Pink 'Un Days* London 1924
FRANK BROWNE *Sport From Within* London 1952
T. H. BROWNE *A History of the English Turf* 2 Vols. London 1931
CAPTAIN X *Tales of The Turf* London N.D.
SIR GEORGE CHETWYND Bt *Racing Reminiscences and Experiences of
  The Turf* London 1891
WILLIAM DAY *Reminiscences of William Day of Danebury* London 1886
HENRY HALL DIXON ('The Druid') *The Post and The Paddock* London
  1856
  Silk and Scarlet London 1859
STEPHEN DONOGHUE *Just My Story* London N.D.
  Donoghue Up London 1938
E. E. DORLING *Epsom and the Dorlings* London 1939
ROGER FULFORD *Votes for Women* London 1957
SYDNEY GALTREY *Memoirs of A Racing Journalist* London 1934
QUINTIN GILBEY *Champions All* London 1971
ROBERT GRAVES *They Hanged My Saintly Billy* London 1957
GEORGE GREVILLE *The Greville Memoirs* (abridged edition) London
  1963
GEORGE HODGMAN *Sixty Years on The Turf* London 1901
SIDNEY JACKSON *Rufus Isaacs, First Marquess of Reading* London 1936
JACK JARVIS *They're Off* London 1969
RAE JOHNSTONE *The Rae Johnstone Story* London 1958
CHESTER KIRBY *The English Country Gentleman* London N.D.

215

G.H.KNOTT *The Trial of William Palmer* (Notable English Trials Series) London 1912

DOROTHY LAIRD *Royal Ascot* London 1976

THE HON GEORGE LAMBTON *Men and Horses I Have Known* London 1924

LADY SARAH LENNOX *Life and Letters* London 1901

MARCHIONESS OF LONDONDERRY *Henry Chaplin, A Memoir* London 1926

ALAN MACEY *The Romance of The Derby Stakes* London N.D.

MARCUS MARSH *Racing With The Gods* London 1968

RICHARD MARSH *A Trainer to Two Kings* London 1925

EDWARD MOORHOUSE *The Romance of The Derby* 2 Vols. London 1908

ROGER MORTIMER *The Jockey Club* London 1958
  The Encyclopaedia of Flat Racing London 1971
  The History of the Derby Stakes (revised edition) London 1973
    with Richard Onslow and Peter Willett *Biographical Encyclopaedia of British Flat Racing* London 1978

PRISCILLA NAPIER *The Sword Dance* London 1967

NIMROD *The Chace, The Road and The Turf* London 1927

WILTON J. OLDHAM *The Ismay Line* London 1961

RICHARD ONSLOW *The Heath and The Turf* London 1971

VINCENT ORCHARD *The Derby Stakes 1900-1953* London 1954

SQUIRE OSBALDESTON *Autobiography* London 1926

DUKE OF PORTLAND *Memories of Hunting and Racing* London 1935

JOHN PORTER *Kingsclere* London 1896
  John Porter of Kingsclere London 1919

ANTONIA RAEBURN *Militant Suffragettes* London 1973

GORDON RICHARDS *My Story* London 1955

GILES ST AUBYN *Infamous Victorians* London 1971

ARTHUR J. SARL *Horses, Jockeys and Crooks* London 1935

MICHAEL SETH-SMITH *Lord Paramount of the Turf* London 1971
  Steve, The Life and Times of Steve Donoghue London 1974

FRANK SILTZER *Newmarket, Its Sport and Personalities* London 1923

CHARLIE SMIRKE *Finishing Post* London 1960

THORMANBY *Famous Racing Men* London 1882
  Kings of The Turf London 1898

VARIOUS *British Sports and Sportsmen* 3 Vols. London 1920
  The British Turf and The Men Who Made It London 1906

Bibliography

VERBATIM *Report of the Trial of William Palmer* London 1856
C. A. VOIGHT *Famous Gentlemen Riders At Home and Abroad* London (N.D.)
TOMMY WESTON *My Racing Life* London 1952

Newspapers and Periodicals

Baileys Magazine
Bells Life
The Field
Illustrated Sporting and Dramatic News
The Morning Chronicle and Public Advertiser
The Morning Post
The Racing Calendar
Sporting Life
The Sportsman
The Times
The Winning Post

Index

219